For permission requests, please contact the author directly at:
Loosen Your White Collar
Melissa Anzman
melissa@loosenyourwhitecollar.com
http://loosenyourwhitecollar.com

Contents

Hi, I'm Melissa Anzman and I'm a former Human Resources corporate drone turned Founder and career strategist at Loosen Your White Collar. After spending more than ten years in various HR environments and being frustrated with every job that I had along the way, I finally took the leap and left my high-paying corporate job to follow my own dreams. Part of that dream is to help you find your next job by sharing all of my Human Resources insider information and ensure you put your best foot forward so you can land your next corporate gig.

Chapter 1 - Introduction

* * *

Have You Ever Had These Challenges?

I get so many emails from friends, family members and clients asking why they are not getting any traction from the multiple online applications they are submitting. Or wondering why they made it through several rounds of interviews, but have not yet been extended the offer of their dreams. Perhaps even more devastating, they have been unemployed or underemployed for more than six months or have been told that they were not a good fit for their dream job. It happens all of the time.

You apply and apply into cyberspace, never knowing if your resume is ever getting into the hands of the right person. Or that interview that you finally scored results in radio silence from the company. With so many qualified people applying for the same job, it seems even harder now than ever before to get your foot in the door at a new company.

It is happening everywhere. It is harder to stand out from an overqualified crowd. But what if I told you that there is a different way? It is slightly more time-intensive up front, but the payoff will come faster and be better than you ever imagined. I have been on both sides of the fence – I have searched for many, many corporate jobs and I have also hired for many, many corporate jobs. And I am eager to share with you what I have learned along the way from both perspectives.

Me, Too

It all started when I graduated college and I decided I was going to move to New York (this was December 2001 mind you, right after 9/11/01). I did not have a job solidified. In fact, I did not have a single lead, but I was confident that it would all work itself out (ignorance is bliss, no?). I believed in my skill set and my capability to interview well and start at the bottom. I was clueless about landing a job. You should see how hilarious my first resume was! But I secured a job the second day after I arrived through some contacts and connections along the way.

Just like you, I have had my fair share of job searches. In fact, I was a serial job hopper most of my career – but I learned something about my job hunt strategy early on. I did not struggle to land jobs; in fact, I usually received multiple offers during each job hunt. I had no idea that this was not the "norm;" in fact, I was kept in the dark about my job hunting "special sauce" until the third job I landed. I thought that having multiple offers happened to everyone (ah, to be young).

My friends started coming to me for job hunting advice. And pretty soon, they were all landing new jobs and attracting multiple offers. It turned into a fun challenge amongst us –who landed the best job, in the shortest amount of time. And this was all *before* I started working in HR. You can only imagine how those questions ramped up then!

My Search for a Solution

My advice and approach worked for so many people, but I could not figure out exactly HOW. I was successful in helping others land their own dream jobs, but it was not until I was working on the other side of the fence in Human Resources that I was able to identify why my approach was working. I evaluated what was working for me and what was failing for all of the others I had helped then cross-referenced my experiences with the recruiting process and tools. And finally all of the puzzle pieces connected – and my Land a Job framework was created.

Results

Since putting my solution in place, I have been privileged to work with hundreds of people to help them land better jobs. And let me tell you, there was definitely resistance along the way from some of them! But they stuck it out and implemented my plan from start to finish, and many of them ended up received competing offers.

One of my favorite examples is from a former client named Chris. He was resistant the entire way – in fact, during our first conversation he told me "I don't need anyone else to help me with my resume, so I'm not really sure what you can do to help. I have been updating it on my own for years." I was confused – after all, he contacted me. But as we continued to chat, he told me that he had never landed the job he most desired, he could not even get his foot in the door. So I asked him to work with me… to put a little trust in my experience and see where it goes. He had nothing to lose, so away we went. And for the first time in his career, he received an offer from his dream job – even though he fought the process from Facebook to Negotiation, his results were outstanding and he ended up becoming one of my biggest client-referral sources!

Another example of resistance came from a relative (no, I will *not* disclose his/her name). They absolutely refused to make the changes I continually provided to their search process – from search sites to resume updates. But they kept coming back to me asking me why they were not getting any traction. I convinced them to just try my process for five jobs – that is it, not a huge commitment in time or process. And see what happens… You guessed it! They received interview requests from a few of the five jobs in "our batch." Needless to say they updated their job-landing process to my methods, going forward.

Whether you need help understanding what goes on behind the scenes in the recruiting process, figuring out the best jobs to which you should apply to, updating your resume appropriately, my system works and it is applicable to you regardless of where you are in the job hunt process.

Old World

When I first started hunting for the secret to my job-landing success, I read as many books and blogs about job hunting that I could get my hands on. Some of the most popular methods and advice that they shared was from over 20 years ago!!! The recruiting field and ways to land a job have changed dramatically in the past two years alone. I could not understand why people were still seeking job advice from people who last hunted 20 years ago (or more).

This book provides you with what works in today's market – how to compete with other qualified candidates, how to leverage social media appropriately, how to communicate with the HR workforce of today, and how to stand out in the information-cluttered world. And it is coming from someone who is just like YOU – I have been there, done that, struggled along the way, and I have also been the person who hired you. This is not your parents' job hunt, and this is not what your college taught you about getting a job. This is pure experience from both sides of the coin, warts and all.

Ready to go after that job and put in the work that it takes to actively *land* a job, not passively hunt for one? Then this book is for you – and I cannot wait to guide you on your journey.

It's time to stop job-hunting and start job-landing!

Chapter 2 – Get Your Social Media in Order

* * *

Social Media is an important tool to help you land a new job, but it can just as easily be the barrier for you to be looked over. We have become so used to having our lives documented for everyone to see, that when it comes time to look for a new challenge, we forget about everything we have already put out into the world… until you are Googled by a hiring manager. Before you make one edit to your resume, before you start hitting the apply button, before you go and network the heck out of yourself, you need to get your social media situation in check.

Google

Before a recruiter or hiring manager schedules your first phone interview, he/she will Google you. Just like you Google every new person you meet, the official gate keepers at companies are not going to let just anyone into their recruiting process, and Google is the first stop on their investigative journey.

The first two pages of your Google results are the most important. It is very rare that the hiring manager or recruiter will look past page two, unless you are being considered for the top job, or in a highly visible position. Having two pages of clean results should be sufficient for most jobs, but it may take more effort than you think, to fully "clean" those two pages, especially if you have not been worried about your online presence before today. The goal is simple – your Google results should be an accurate representation of who you are, with all of the bad stuff left out. It should be the best you, you can present to the world.

Start by doing a search of your own name, I like the quote method such as typing into Google: "Melissa Anzman" and seeing what comes up. This will quickly isolate the best results for you. When looking at the first two pages of results, keep an eye out for the following red flags:

- Anything related or posted from Facebook
- Pictures (be sure to check the Google images section!), as in out-having-fun pictures
- Court cases or legal information
- False information or accusations
- Negative stories or reviews

Those are broad flags, but should provide a good framework of what needs to be removed from Google instantly. You know, all of the things you want to hide from your mom or grandma should be hidden from potential companies as well.

Cleaning up your online image can take some time, but is doable. On Google, you can request link removals through their site and also through the offending link itself. But remember, that once it is on the web, it is there forever – caches live on my friend. If you have significant clean-up to do such as false information posted about you, detrimental photos that will not disappear, and other potentially damaging links, I would recommend researching online reputation companies who can assist you throughout the process. A good place to start is a company called Reputation.com.

Facebook

Ah, Facebook. The bane of a job seeker's existence and you probably do not even know it. If I have said this once, I have said it a thousand times – for the love of Nancy, change your Facebook settings to PRIVATE and share your updates with your friends only. Why is it so important that your updates are private? Remember that Google thing above – everything that is posted on Facebook, your pictures, your comments, your status updates, are fed through Google and other search engines to live indefinitely on the web if your status is public. Um, can you imagine all of the embarrassing things that will haunt you years to come?

So go update your privacy settings now – I will wait. It must feel a bit odd not having your whole world hanging out there, but trust me – it will greatly benefit you in your job hunt. Be sure to check your privacy settings each month as Facebook is known to make updates to your settings, which tend to get lost in translation.

And now it is time to clean up your Facebook friends. I am still not sure how people have 500+ friends, or how you even know that many people, but if you are serious about your job hunt, you will need to review who your friends are before moving forward. Don't worry – your badge of pride for having the most friends will not suffer much.

And a little note about what is already up on Facebook… If it is already there, it is available online. Not to fret – go back and de-tag your name/face in photos that are compromising and "delete" any posts or updates that are unbecoming of a job-landing professional. Do the best you can about what is already posted, but remember that moving forward and having everything squared away now is what is important.

Everything that you post on Facebook is visible to your network, so if you are posting about your current job frustrations, your job hunting successes and failures, your friends can see it. And you definitely do NOT want your boss knowing what you are up to at this point in the game. The most important people to take off of your friend list are your current work colleagues, especially your boss. I never advise to have work colleagues as your friends on Facebook until *after* you have left the company, but if you are already friends with a lot of your work friends, be sure to de-friend the following: your boss (no negotiation here); anyone you work with who you would consider nosy or a gossip; your boss's assistant (um, I would remove anyone's assistant); any peers who you do not consider your confidants; and your work "rivals."

Cleaning up your friends is a good start, but you will also need to be more careful going forward about what kind of status updates you post. It will take some serious self-control if you are a constant sharer, but I promise it will pay off. The less information you have out there, the “safer” your Facebook environment is for your job hunt.

In addition to cleaning out your friends and curbing your status update enthusiasm, it’s time to edit yourself and the content that is already posted. Review all pictures that you are in, have posted, or were tagged – and remove/delete/de-tag all of the photos that are inappropriate or embarrassing. Right after Googling you, the hiring manager is going to hop onto Facebook and search you. In fact, I have known a few hiring managers that become a bit like Facebook stalkers. Secure your page and remove offending content.

LinkedIn

I could probably create a whole book on how to prepare your LinkedIn profile for your job hunt. But that could be a bit…boring. Instead, I will cover the most important updates that you need to make to prepare for your job search. This could be one of your biggest tools in helping you secure a job – do not overlook LinkedIn’s power and influence, second only to your resume materials. LinkedIn helps recruiters and hiring managers instantly find out significant information about you, in an unobtrusive way. It can provide a more robust view of who you are as a candidate, your experience, who you know, and how influential you are. A lot to learn from one website.

One of the most common mistakes that I have found is candidates not completing their entire LinkedIn profile. If you are seeking a job, this is a non-negotiable. You absolutely must take an hour or so to complete each and every section, including uploading an appropriate photo (more on this in a minute).

Basic things to update immediately:

- Your profile settings to private (and remove visible settings from “show all network activity” to “hide all activity.”

- Update your headline – change this from your current position, to something that will immediately capture a hiring manager who is looking for your skillset. Focus on your talents and skills, instead of a specific job. For example, instead of saying "Social Media Manager" change your headline to "Experienced Social Media Community Liaison."
- Contact information should be professional, even if you typically use a hotmail account for your log-ins. The email that you have as your log-in is the same one that employers see, so be sure to change this to your professional account (one that has your name in it!).
- Update your profile titles and dates of each position to match exactly with your resume titles and dates. Clean it up and eliminate all of the confusion.

And to ensure that you update your entire LinkedIn profile appropriately, be sure to review my step-by-step guide.

Position Information

Every position you have held within the previous 10 years should be included in your profile and should be 100% accurate and legit. You should post your official title, actual job duties and accomplishments, and so on. LinkedIn is NOT the place to exaggerate or include a white lie because you will be caught and it will be devastating (and embarrassing as hell). In the job duties/description section, do not simply copy/paste the information from your resume. Unlike the bullets from your resume, this section should provide more context of your overall position and responsibilities, not only your grand accomplishments. Recruiters will be looking for the level of influence of your position, the value you delivered to your company, and your official responsibilities and title. You should do a little bragging here, but be concise about it. Include all of the "wow factors" from each job, and then show how you delivered in at each company.

Photo Area

This is the one and only place that it is appropriate for you to use a photo of yourself. But do so, carefully. Including a picture that you feel is representative of who you are as a WORKING PROFESSIONAL is critical, but it could be a double-edged sword. Your photo is helpful to the recruiter in placing a face with the name of stand-out candidates and also allows him/her to get a feel for your personality and potential culture fit. But recruiters are people, so there is always room for error, including the unfortunate potential for discrimination.

Lessons in photo discrimination:

- **Do not include any pictures of you in a casual setting.** I have seen several candidates who have a photo of them on the beach, on a boat, hanging out on the couch, or other similar "hanging out" photos. While these are not necessarily the worst pictures, they should absolutely be avoided. The general feeling you present is one of carefreeness, casualness, not taking your job hunt seriously. This is a professional networking site, and the people who will most likely be seeking you out are Human Resources professionals. They want to find a polished match to your resume, so kick the casual off-the-cuff photo to the wayside.
- **Do not include your family.** Sometimes it is unclear who in the picture is the job hunter, but more importantly, you have no idea what personal subconscious biases the recruiter may have or what they are looking for. Perhaps it is a position that requires a lot of travel – if your picture includes your family, you may be automatically disqualified for "not being able to travel." This can be exacerbated, particularly when young children are included.
- **Age discrimination.** I wish I could say that this is not a possibility of posting your picture, but it absolutely is something you should be thinking about – young or old. Most importantly, you want to show yourself as a

professional, regardless of your age. To combat looking “too young,” I would recommend your photo/headshot be taken with a plain background with you wearing a suit or blazer. If you are on the other side of the equation, worried about looking to old, here’s what I would recommend. First, be clear about the type of job and level you are going to go after. If it’s a high-level position at a larger company, absolutely keep the suit on. If you want to aim for a younger, hip, fun company, try going with a business casual presentation. Above all else, make sure that your haircut and color, make-up, and general presentation is work and age appropriate (I hate that I have to add this).

Review Your Contacts

Being really connected on LinkedIn is a good thing, but things can get dicey when you are connected with your current boss and work friends, particularly any members of the Human Resources team. When you are actively seeking a new position, your LinkedIn account will be jumping with activity – inviting new friends, applying for jobs, researching people, looking up companies, updating your profile, adding new skills, and so on. While you are able to manage who sees these types of updates through your privacy settings, certain things will come through and you could easily raise a few “I’m looking for a new job” flags.

For the time being, I recommend removing your current boss and the office gossips from your network – and then you can add them back later if you want. But this will help eliminate some of the online paranoia that comes when leveraging LinkedIn appropriately.

Why is This So Important?

Oh, good – I thought you would never ask. Other than being your calling card for any and all recruiters, hiring managers and companies, your LinkedIn profile is also an application tool. Bet you have no idea what the recruiting interface looks like, so here it is!

When you apply for a position, here is what the recruiter sees when they log-on to LinkedIn. Note that the only info they see is your name, current headline, location and area of expertise, and your contact info. That's… it.

Featured Applicants on page one:

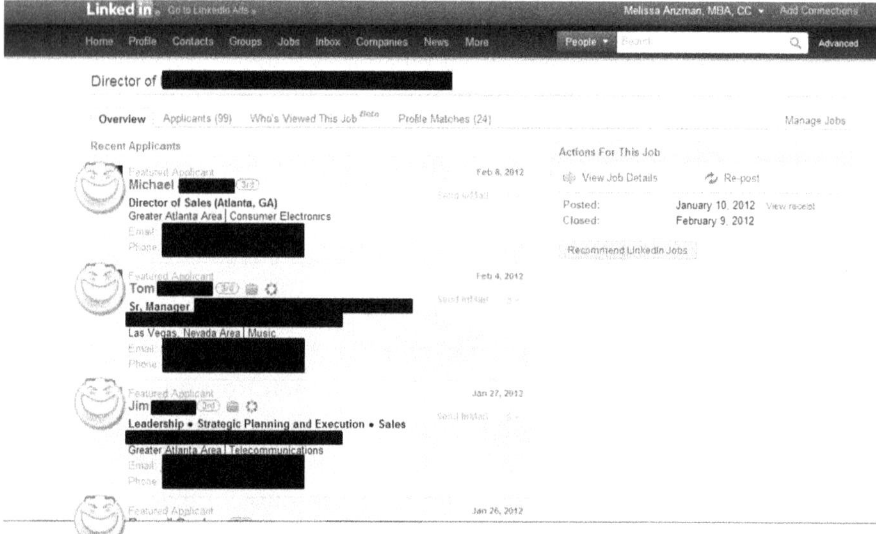

General applicants, including the options for sorting candidates:

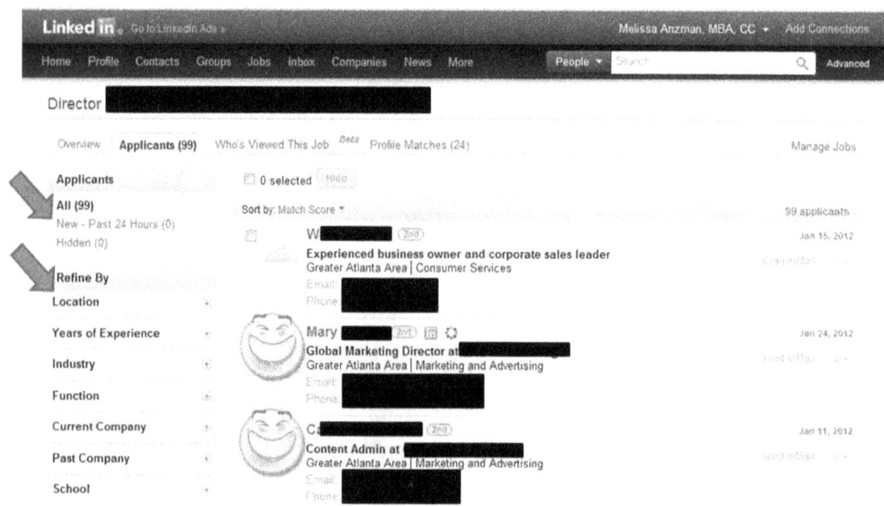

Some recruiters also have candidates' information emailed to their inbox. This is critical and directly applies to the guidance from above about everything "looking" right and matching your resume. The email contains the same information as the dashboard, except that your resume is attached to the email.

Hopefully seeing some examples of how you are presented to your potential employers, will help you understand how to create a more impressive LinkedIn profiles and why they are so darn important in today's hiring process.

Twitter, Instagram, Pinterest, etc.

I am sure that by the time this is published there will be another new social media sharing site that I am just too old to know about, but the same rules apply to all of them. Unlink all of these accounts from your LinkedIn profile, at a minimum.

Did you know that if your Twitter account is connected, every single thing that you tweet is also shared on your LinkedIn newsfeed? I had a candidate who used her twitter account for her social life only (absolutely fine in general), but had it connected to her LinkedIn profile. You know what her tweets said? "Picking up some beers; had a great time getting wasted; see this pic of me with my newest conquest;" and a few more things unsuitable for the general public. And this was all on her newsfeed on LinkedIn.

Instagram and Pinterest are similar – if you utilize these social media sites to connect with friends, versus having it as a part of your overall brand, disconnect them from LinkedIn and be careful about what you post, just in case.

Chapter 3 – Be Clear About the Job You Are Seeking

* * *

Your job hunt is not a "free for all" hunting operation. I know there are a limited number of jobs out there and you may be reaching an "any job will do" mentality, but even in desperation, you need to be very clear about the type of job you are seeking. There is nothing more dreaded to a recruiter than a candidate trying to win the all-around award in Generalism.

I suffered with this syndrome through most of my career – I was open to many different types of jobs, industries, locations, and functions because there were so many things that I enjoyed doing. But I was told time and time again from headhunters that I was a difficult placement because they had no idea where to start for me. They also ran into the confusion over labels that hiring managers love – "Are you an HR professional or a Communications Specialist? I don't understand." People need to label, pigeon-hole and identify each candidate before getting to know them; it helps them identify certain skills needed to succeed in a particular role, as well as help them quickly identify people who belong in the "no" pile.

Generalist versus Specialist

Every 15 years or so, the workforce changes drastically, and what was once considered valuable becomes passé. The debate between being a generalist versus being a specialist is one area of contention that is a consistent contender in this debate. I firmly believe that as a candidate and as an employee, having multiple skills will only help you – which plays to the generalist mentality. However, in today's work environment, being a specialist is what will get you hired.

Being too open or broad in your background and desired position comes across as being desperate and indecisive. Why would any hiring manager choose the person who is wishy-washy about the job over someone who has worked his/her entire life to achieve this exact position? See the difference? This is a huge hurdle for many job seekers and it boils down to being as clear as possible about the position you are seeking, not being a fit for any and every position out there. In other words, having the skills of a jack-of-all-trades is critical, but coming across as a specialist with the skills and experience exactly matching what the company is searching for is a shoe-in for getting hired.

Hint: to a certain degree you can change your specialty for each application. We will discuss how to do that in the next section.

Unemployed?

This is your wake-up call, snap out of it! Not just any job will do, so leave that notion behind. NOW. In fact, this lack of focus and clarity is one of the main reasons you are still unemployed. Your desperation or ambivalence leaves a sour taste in every recruiter's mouth, so it is time to try a new tactic and approach and start specializing.

One of my clients, Brooke, struggled with this for over two years before coming to me – no, you did not read that wrong, she was unemployed for over two years. And she left her previous job by choice! I know, you just gasped a little, didn't you. Anyway, she ended up being unemployed for so long because she was all over the place in the types of jobs she was looking for. One week she applied for sales management jobs, the next week she focused on renewable energy entry-level positions. Then she would try and land entry-level sales representative jobs, and then went on to apply for marketing positions. She was a hot-mess. Hitting up the same companies in significantly different departments created a sense of desperation and lack of direction, which immediately sent warning bells to the recruiters. So it was time to shake it up and try a more focused approach – changing from the generalist "I can do anything just hire me now, thank you" mentality, to a specialist approach of "I am really good at sales and here are my accomplishments."

And you guessed it, she landed a job within her preferred department, Sales, shortly thereafter. Choosing *something* as your specialty will absolutely help you go from unemployed to getting a paycheck faster.

I Don't Freaking Know, Ok?

Decisions, decisions, decisions. Making a choice, especially about what you want your next job or career to be, is not an easy decision. This is the point where many job seekers or employees who are miserable in their current job, simply stop and give up. This is a great procrastination point, I know from my own experience.

Remember – this is not a forever decision. You can absolutely change your focus down the road if you need to, so stop the analysis paralysis and start the decision-making process. Not being sure about what you want your next job to be is not only ok, but it is normal. But you have to figure it out for now, to start marching towards landing your next job. And together, we will find clarity around this decision.

One of the easiest ways to jumpstart your skill search is to hop on a job site like SimplyHired.com and start doing some research. Type in a job title that you think you may be interested in applying for and start looking at the job descriptions. I tend to open around ten at a time in different industries and locations to get a well-rounded view of what a "Marketing Manager" does at various companies. From the open job descriptions, start making a list of your own with the desired skills they are asking for.

Once you have compiled the skill list, use the following template to determine your own skills:

Skill from Job Description	Do I possess this skill now?	Do I excel at this skill?	Do I want to use this skill going forward?

Things to Consider

Non-negotiables

We all have them, the list of things that a company could not pay you enough to endure. And we also have things that we need to make it worth our time. Both sides of this coin are your non-negotiables and are your starting points to find your clarity. The critical thing to remember when determining these things is that they are NEEDS, not wants. If you are going on a camping trip, your non-negotiables will probably be food, water, and some sort of shelter. That fantastic air mattress and portable TV, you can do without. Think along the same lines when creating your list of non-negotiables.

Questions to Ask:

1. **Do you have a specific skill set that you enjoy and have honed throughout your career that you absolutely must utilize in your next job?**

   For instance, I have a very unique niche skill set in employee communications. Being in a job where I do not get to flex this muscle at all would be a non-negotiable. I love the art of communication, I love being able to help others interact with their employees better, and enjoy the freedom that this knowledge set provides me.

2. **What is your pay threshold, the very bottom of the ladder of which you need to make to cover your expenses?**

   If you *need* to make six-figures to cover all of your expenses including your mortgage, child support, and so on, then going after an entry-level position is probably not the smartest idea. We would all like to make as much money as we possibly can, but this is about determining what the bottom threshold is, so you are clear during your job hunt.

3. **What daily actions will you absolutely not do?**

   My friend Paul refuses to make copies or send out office mail. Absolutely refuses – apparently it comes from a stint in publicity when he had to make thousands of copies of marketing materials each week and mail them out, snail-mail style. So any position that requires these skills from him are not jobs that he will pursue. **Be careful not to rule all of the annoying things out**, there will always be some of that – but be sure to include the things that make you cringe just thinking about them.

What are you trying to fix, escape or improve?

If you are looking for a job, you are definitely looking for something *better*. A job that will be *more or less* of something for you. Whether that is fulfillment, enjoyment, money, power, responsibility, and so on. Simply thinking or wishing that your next job will alleviate all of the issues that your current job provides will not solve your problems. You need to be clear on what you are trying to fix, escape, or improve upon in your next role.

Maybe there are small issues that are fixable such as the décor, or perhaps there are larger issues such as the hierarchy and decision-making process. Either way, figure out why you are seeking something new and what it is you would need improved in your next role, to stop the cycle of job jumping.

Exercise:

It is time to determine all of the things that you need to leave behind! For the next 30 minutes, bullet-out (a.k.a. write down) all of the things that you hope you do not stumble across in your new job – big, small and everything in between. Be sure to include all of the things that you would like to see improved in your next role. Do not move from your seat until 30 minutes are up (I'm watching you).

Ideal conditions

There is not one dream job out there for you, instead there are several different jobs that will mostly match what you are looking for and make work an enjoyable experience. So why not start thinking about those ideal conditions that would make your new job *that much* better? Below are some questions to get you started. The key here is to answer these questions realistically. Yes, we would all love for our commutes to be less than 10 minutes away, our hours to be from 9 a.m. – 5 p.m. every day, and to have an extensive pension plan. But that job may not exist, so answer the below questions with a desired range in mind of acceptability.

Questions to Ask:

1. What type of company do you want to work at?
2. What size of company do you thrive in?
3. What are you willing to sacrifice – in other words, what is your balance scale?
4. What type of commute are you willing to put up with?
5. What hours do you want to work?
6. What's the level of responsibility or demand that would fit within your ideal job?
7. Is there a specific department that you want to be a part of?
8. Are there special benefits that you want to have?

Reality Check Yourself, Yo

And the part that you thought I would forget, huh? YOU are the most important piece of this puzzle – your existent skill set is critical in determining what the best specialized job is for you. This is your reality check. Why do some people land jobs consistently and others do not? Because they are realistic about their own skill set and abilities and then use their skills to their advantage.

Most likely you have a baseline for the skills that you possess – the things that you are currently doing in your job, classes that you excelled in at school, or things that you have pursued in your free time. These are all great starting points, but do not sell yourself short! You have so many skills that you are able to leverage when seeking a new position, all of which will help cement your candidacy as a specialist, and set you apart from others during the recruiting process.

Start the List

1. What was your college major? Did you excel in those courses?
2. What is your favorite part of your current job?
3. In your performance reviews, what tends to consistently stand out?
4. Is there a particular department that you are interested in or work exceptionally well with?
5. What do your outside-of-work "passions" have in common?
6. What is your favorite pastime (or guilty pleasure) and why?
7. Are you big picture person, or more interested in details?
8. Do you consider yourself more practical or more of a dreamer?
9. Math and science, or English and History?
10. What types of things do you love to do in your daily job? What do you hate?

To dig deeper about your skills and strengths, here are a few recommended resources:

- *Strengths Finder 2.0* by Tom Rath: This book comes with an interactive quiz that helps you determine your strengths within a work environment and then also details how each strength can be utilized appropriately. The premise of this book is that once you know your strengths, you should *only* be doing things that play to those strengths.
- America's Career InfoNet: This is an online resource sponsored by the U. S. Department of Labor, Employment and Training Administration. It is a good resource to help you find skills that may be hidden.

Here is the reality check: you are most likely self-inflating your true skill level. I know, I burst your bubble just a little there. Knowing what your skills *are* is the first part of the equation; you must also understand your skill **level** for each of those skills. This is the part that I have found trips up each and every person. While we can easily be our own worst critics, during the job hunt we are striving to grow and be better, so our perspective gets a bit… off.

Have you ever applied for a job that is well above the level you are currently at title-wise, and then was upset about not getting the position? Or perhaps you are "wrongly passed over" for internal promotions? Or you are simply not getting *any* bites during your application process? If any of the above has happened, then you need a bit of a refresher of your skill level.

Skill-Level Job Title Handy Tool

In order to help you better evaluate your own skills with a bit more objectivity, I have put together the tool below. It is important to note that each industry is different, but for the majority of large companies out there, the below guide will mostly be applicable. I know that your knee-jerk reaction may be to roll your eyes or scream that I am wrong about the info provided. I am fully prepared for the angry emails. ;) It is difficult to see past our own ambition and desires to mold into a "corporate hierarchy," hopefully this will provide some transparency for you.

And the dreaded conversation about "the job description says I need five years of experience, but I only have three" can be avoided. In general terms, the number of years' experience that is posted, is a *guideline,* not a hard-and-fast rule. However, if they are asking for 10 years of experience and you only have five years of experience, you are most likely not qualified for that position.

Years of WORK Experience (in an office environment)	Title Correlation
0 – 2 Years	• Assistant • Associate • Coordinator
2 – 4 Years	• Specialist • Coordinator • Analyst • Account Executive (sales or customer service position) • Representative
4 – 6 Years	• Associate Manager • Senior Specialist • Assistant VP (financial industry) • Supervisor • Account Manager (sales or customer service position) • 5+ years - Manager
6 – 8 Years	• Manager • Senior Manager • Consultant
8 – 10 Years	• Senior Manager • Associate Director • Director • Advisor/Principal • Vice President (financial industry)

Another thing to add, your advanced degree does not automatically move you up the scale. I know, they lied to you in grad school, but that is ok – it will probably pay off for you down the road when you have six plus years of experience. The above relates to actual office work experience – not internships, not schooling, not working for Mom and Dad, not being unemployed, not age. Only work experience. Capice?

So if you currently have three to five years of experience and are consistently applying to jobs at the manager level and above, you need to knock that off right now. You do not have the skill level to perform well in those jobs. If there is a dream job out there that you absolutely must apply for at the manager level in this example, apply – but know that you would be a *stretch* hire in that position, so do not let disappointment set-in too much.

Are you officially level-set and clear about the job you are going after?

Chapter 4 – Your Resume

* * *

This section alone is the subject of many long books and ramblings around the web. This will not be another long drawn out "how to" guide, but it will be the most comprehensive and definitive guide from a hiring manager and Human Resources perspective of what to worry about and what to skip in your overall resume materials presentation. People do still judge a book by its cover even if we all know that we should not, but most hiring managers do not have the time or insight to skip this logic and dig deeper about each and every candidate.

Do not underestimate the power of a complete, well-designed and smartly-worded resume, cover letter and overall presentation materials. These tools are far from perfect, but they are the "currency" in which many companies use to select candidates. Your "package" is essential for success landing a new job.

One note of challenge to your ego… I get resistance often from my clients, friends and family members about resume advice and guidance I provide (this happens to all resume writers, I have checked with several). Often the response is something like "well I know best" or "that may be true for X job, but I am looking for Y" or "this has worked in the past for me" or the general "I know better than you, so there" arguments. Now is the time to check your ego at the door. You have not been presenting yourself correctly or you would have landed your dream job already. You are an expert in certain things and I would never be expected to do your expert job at the level that you do it, so I am not sure why the art and science of resume materials is a different beast.

Here is what I do know: I have been doing this for a long time and have reviewed tens of thousands of resumes and have hired (or not hired) just as many candidates. I know what I look for, I know what online application programs look for, and I know what has consistently worked for my clients. That is what I am sharing with you – whether you take the advice or not, is completely up to you (but I do hope that you are open to it!).

Pick Your Specialization

Today is all about specialization – you want to be an expert in one thing, so that your value comes across as direct as possible. For the rest of this book, you will need to focus on ONE job target; one job title/position/family to focus on, to create your resume materials around. Once you have put everything together using these exercises and steps for one position, you will easily be able to replicate it for any other job title or position that you seek.

Being focused on just one target job is a bit restricting. I shared with you earlier how I have always been a "jack-of-all-trades" and how frustrating it is to have to narrow down my skills to meet only one job, but it has consistently paid off and I know it will do the same for you. Remember that people want to hire experts. Expertise is easier to present when you present yourself in a focused manner.

Recently, an online friend of mine, Nadine, reached out to me for a "business proposition Skype date." I love meeting new online friends via Skype and the business proposition part sounded… interesting, so I decided to meet with her to find out more. When we started talking, she told me what she did for a living and I swear my head was spinning (thankfully we were only on voice chat). Here is how she introduced herself: "I do some freelance writing, I'm a blogger, a many times over failed entrepreneur, graphic designer, and marketer."

Mind you, I only knew her in the freelance writing capacity, so I was a bit stunned that she introduced herself as an expert in so many things. Added to that, her business proposition was about a potential entrepreneurial partnership with her, with her focus on design. Um, wait what? All I could think during the entire conversation was… she is a many times over *failed* entrepreneur and she is asking me to partner with her, and she has no experience doing her side of the partnership, oh and she has design skills? I have obviously come across many skillset introductions throughout my career, but this one stands out to me as the most jumbled one in history. I am sure that she has great skills in each one of those categories, but her lack of focus when presenting herself not only confused me but also made me question if she was an expert in anything at all.

Part 1: 30,000 Foot View

What is Your Resume?

We all *know* what a resume is – it is a piece of paper that includes all of your contact information, your work experience, your education information, and your skills. And that is where we typically stop, but a resume is so much more. But your resume can be magic. (I know, I just stepped into the woo-woo realm, which we all know is *not* me at all – so listen up). It should be the best representation of who you are as a person, what your character is, what skills and accomplishments you value, and should scream why you are the best candidate for the job.

Your resume should be screaming "choose me, don't pass up an offer this good" to every recruiter that sees it. Landing a job is the process of you selling yourself (not your soul, don't worry) – and your resume is what gets your phone call answered and sets you up to close the deal.

Sales for Non-Salesmen

When I recruit for Sales positions, I never have a hard time finding "maybe" candidates – their resumes are usually polished, it is clear what position they are seeking, and I know exactly what the sales professional has accomplished. I do not have the same experience in other types of jobs? Why? Because sales people are innately selling themselves through their resume. It is probably not conscious, but since it is a part of who they are at their core, it comes across in everything they do. It is time to start selling yourself!

I admit, I am a reluctant salesman. The thought of taking on the sales title makes me feel a little slimy. But approaching my resume materials from a sales perspective and learning tips and tricks from the best resumes I have ever seen has proved valuable when job hunting.

Before you start working on the tactics of your resume, you need to put on your objective sales hat and see how you are advertising yourself. Think critically of your overall package, just as you would when deciding to buy a product or service as a consumer. The bottom line: the candidate who represents him/herself in the best light possible, the one who shows me that they are a perfect match, is the one who gets interviewed.

Am I Selling Myself?

- If you were a consumer, would you buy into the candidate that you are selling?
- Am I engaging the reader from the beginning of each sentence through the end of the page?
- Have I put my best product out there?
- Do I have the *buy now* factor in my materials?

We will walk through the tactics of how to make all of these things happen later on, but you need to start thinking about yourself as a commodity and how to put your best foot forward before going any further. Even if you think nothing you have done is outstanding, you will need to package your experience as a hot ticket.

Issues, Gaps, and Grads

Each person's work experience is vastly different and your resume should be reflective of that, but you also need to address the potential red flags in your resume to create a level playing field. I have included guidance on how to address the most common resume "issues," so you can position yourself properly.

Focus on what steps you took to become a better employee in the future during these "gaps;" what personal and professional development opportunities you explored; and how you kept at it throughout the process. Get the hint? Keep working on yourself so your next employer will **benefit** from your time off.

Periods of Unemployment – Six Months or More (involuntary)

Unfortunately having gaps in your employment due to being laid off or other reasons, is common place today. This used to be a huge red flag for hiring managers, but today it is more likely a yellow flag of caution. First and foremost – do not lie about your employment dates to try and "de-flag" yourself. Lying is bad… ok? You are still a viable candidate with a lot to bring to the table; you just need to present it properly. Here are some things to consider…

- There is no need for you to put on your resume that you were laid off, fired, or any other reason why you were unemployed. That is a distraction that should be avoided.
- Only include truly relevant positions. I have seen people include positions that were unnecessary or fake to try and gobble up the unemployment gaps. For example, do not put down you had your own consulting agency if you did not have any consulting clients.
- Place less emphasis on the dates of employment throughout your resume and more emphasis on your achievements.

Essentially, this is a packaging game and it is time for you to lose the shame. Having involuntary gaps in your employment usually leads to questions about what you did during those times. Be prepared to have something fabulous to talk about during the phone interview.

Larger companies may be a bit more difficult to break into if you have been out of work for some time. So the best companies to aim for are small to mid-sized companies, and it would be even better to aim for a local organization. The more *you* are able to get to know the company and hiring manager, the better your chances are that the company will be sympathetic about your plight and want to hire you.

Periods of Unemployment – Six Months or More (voluntary)

There are some people, myself included, who have taken voluntary time off. Most people have a fantastic story to share about this: traveled the world, wrote a book, pursued a passion, volunteered around the world, and whatever else you can imagine. How you would approach this gap is a bit different than involuntary unemployment.

Depending upon your reason, or perhaps how cool it is, you can include the time gap in your resume. If you were a part of an organization during your time off, you can include that as you would any other job position, or you can place the details in other areas of your resume (profile, skills, summary, etc). But beware – this information is not going to impress everyone. Be cognizant of your company and the audience. For example, if you are applying to Facebook or Google and you took a year off to travel the world and volunteer along the way, this will add more value to your candidacy. However, take that same scenario and apply it to a company like Ernst & Young, and they may see it as a time-waster. Know your audience when including your personal passions and be prepared to tell them what you learned along the way and how it bettered you as a person and employee.

This profile is highly valued by younger companies, particularly online businesses of any size and non-profits. You want to aim for companies that have a large community presence and value self-discovery and the work hard/play hard mentality. But be ready to have a cool reason why you took some time off.

Job Jumper

Hello my friends, you are in good company. And let me also say that job jumpers are more the norm these days than they were when I started looking for jobs! I cannot begin to tell you how many times I was scolded by head hunters about my one year and run philosophy. It annoyed me, it still does because I think you gain so much valuable experience and business acumen from working in different environments, but many hiring managers are still thinking with the mindset from past generations where people stayed with one company their entire lives (can you even imagine that?).

The most important thing about being a job jumper, is owning it. You should not call it out specifically unless they ask you about it, but having varied experiences is a good thing if you play your cards right. You will need to be extra concise about your achievements in your resume and conversation, so that you are highlighting just how great each position was. Have your leaving story prepared and practiced. If you left because you hated your boss, telling that to your potential new boss is a disaster waiting to happen. So thoroughly consider each position and why you wanted to explore a new opportunity – perhaps the new job allowed you to develop more leadership skills; maybe you relocated; or at the very least, you left for a promotional opportunity and more money (just do not use this one for every job). You will be asked and your answer has the capability to vastly sway your candidacy.

Also, you have to be careful about which jobs you include on your resume. Even *I* cringe when I see people going from job to job after three months. See how fine this line is? Consider which jobs you held for at least nine months (hopefully a little longer than that) that provided you with the best learning experiences, and emphasize them on your resume.

Career Changer

I am not sure how this started, but I see many resumes of people trying to change career paths, that do not include anything from their previous career. Did I miss a memo somewhere? You absolutely will need to approach your resume materials differently depending upon the job or career you applying for, but you learned applicable skills in your previous career that you need to take credit for. In fact, highlighting your previous career achievements provides you with a fantastic segue in your resume and during your interviews. You can show how you flex your brain muscles by taking one knowledge set and strategically applying to doing your job in a different environment with even better results.

The important thing to remember is to include the skills that you learned that are directly applicable to the field you are in currently or into which you are seeking to move. For instance, if you were an IT developer in your previous life and are seeking a position in customer service, you would want to include experience that is relevant such as "interacted with clients of various levels; IT troubleshooting; answered the Help Desk as a back-up;" and whatever else there may be. You would leave off things that are only cool to IT people such as: Ruby rails designer; CSS and HTML expert, etc. These things should be included in your skills section, but not featured in your experience section.

The type of company to target in this situation is dependent upon the level you are seeking at your new company. If you are open to taking an entry level position or taking a step back in title to gain relevant experience, then a large company can be a great place for you to get started. They tend to have many positions open at this level and your experience in another field will show that you can be efficient at work and hold down a job. Not to mention that you will be perceived as being easy to train and get up to speed – all awesome things when looking at entry-level positions. If you are trying to get a job in your new career at an even level, be forewarned that this will be a difficult task (not impossible, just hard). The easiest way to target a company in this instance is to go through personal connections – and the company's industry and size will not be as relevant. You will need someone to vouch for you to justify bringing you in at that level. This tends to be easier in a small- to medium-sized business, but it is more about who you know than anything else.

New Graduate

The most important thing you need to know: whatever you learned in college about creating a resume is wrong. I cannot tell you the last time I saw a new grad's resume that hit the marks when following college guidance. Clearly more colleges need to hire me to teach this course. Essentially, you do have a slight disadvantage being that you do not have any "real world work experience" yet. But that does not mean that you should fluff up your resume with complete crap (which I see all the time). If you have had paying jobs in college (leave your high school jobs off completely) or even internships, those should be included and highly emphasized. The better you can show your work ethic, and entry-level skills that you have gained, the better. We are looking for quality over quantity. Your resume should absolutely not be longer than one page. Period.

And for goodness sakes – I do not care about the classes that you took! Take that crap off your resume immediately. The only time that this *might* be something of interest is if you had a very specialized niche class that is 100% applicable to the job you are seeking. Although I am having a hard time thinking of an example, perhaps a specialized science field? Otherwise, you should ***show*** people on your resume that you have experience in the skills you learned in class. You can also provide supportive information in the education section if needed.

The world is your oyster, my friend. Large companies are admittedly a crap shoot for you. If they have a huge campus recruiting presence, then your chances of landing a job decrease slightly. But if you went to what is considered a good school and did well, you will have a chance. I have found that small- to medium-sized businesses are great for new grads to gain some experience and sometimes get paid even more than a large company (since so many new grads want to work at large corporations, the demand is high). Try and match the company culture to what you are looking for, but know that unless you are an absolute phenom and/or created enormous buzz while you were still in school, joining a company like Google without any experience will be difficult (unless you were part of their campus recruiting program).

Fit Your Background to the Company

Each company has its own unique characteristics and personality which is commonly referred to as culture. If you fully understand the culture of a company before you submit your application, you will have a greater chance at landing a job. So many people simply apply to any open job without truly thinking through what type of company they are trying to get into. For instance, it is "cool" to work at companies like Google, Facebook, Apple, and so on. There is a wow factor inherently built in to positions at these companies. But if your profile and work history do not line-up with what these company cultures are looking for, you will never get your foot in the door.

For example, companies like Google and Facebook would value the resume and experience from a strategic job jumper, whereas a company such as MorganStanleySmithBarney, would be concerned by the same resume. This is because the culture at these companies is vastly different. At Google, innovation is critical and valued and that plays into the skills you learn when job jumping: agility, navigating new landscapes, getting up to speed quickly, thinking outside of the box, and so on. At MorganStanleySmithBarney, they value industry experience and deep-rooted connections which do not come about through job jumping.

Not every company is for every person, even if *you* think it is. Especially if you are cold-applying to a position (as in, you do not know someone personally on the hiring team). Consider the size, type and reputation of a company before applying and be sure that your own resume reflects the type of employee they value to increase your chances of getting hired.

Part 2: Practical Tactical Application

Now that you have your strategy in place, you can get to work at building your resume itself. The most important advice I can give when approaching your resume is **SHOW, don't tell**. A great resume should take you a considerable amount of time to complete – it is not easy to compile your accomplishments from each experience and also craft your message in a way that speaks to the hiring manager. If you have only spent one hour on your resume materials, I can assure you that you are not doing it correctly.

Layout Woes

I must receive at least one email per day asking me if it is ok to have a resume that is longer than one page. I am guessing that back in the day when people hand-delivered or snail-mailed resumes, one piece of paper was more than enough clutter for a recruiter to manage, and so the one page limit was created. That is not the case today, for the most part. So to answer the length question once and for all…

If you have worked for five years or less, your resume MUST remain with a one page resume. Your recruiter will not read the second page. Keep it short – at five years of work experience (in the real world) and under, you're still a newbie, so please do not include every single thing you've ever done at a job**. If you have worked for more than five years, cap it off at two pages.** With rare exception (technical fields for instance), at two pages you either have the recruiter's interest or you have lost it – if they are truly interested in what you did 15 years ago, they will be sure to ask you about during your interview. Five pages of resume babble does not help the recruiter get a better grasp on your expertise, it just firmly puts you in the "no" pile.

I Object, Your Honor

This may be controversial, but I am not a fan of having an objective in your resume. More times than not, the objective will count you OUT of the running, versus helping your cause. Since you applied to a job opening, the recruiter is assuming your objective is to get a job – that job specifically. If you say anything other than that it is not adding any value. The most common mistake I have found is people stating their objective for a different type of job than the one the applied to. For example, "I'd like to obtain a job in sales," when they applied for a marketing role. Remove it altogether and get yourself some more space on your resume.

General Look and Feel

The new cool thing is to have a super-designed pretty resume that helps you stand out. A few notes on this… first, if you are using a template that you found online, many others are using the same one (even those crazy-ridiculous color wheel resumes), so you are not standing out so much as you are telling me where you found your template. Second, the highly-designed resumes do not always read well in the Applicant Tracking programs and they most definitely do not capture the verbiage well through those programs. Third, I hate to admit it but many recruiters are still "old school" in resume thinking – a document that is easy to read with strong delivery of words, is more important than how visually interesting it is.

Having a well-designed resume is important for all applicants, but your freedom to make an impact with the design is varied based on the type of position you are applying to. I have recruited for graphic designers in the past and their first test was the look and feel of their resume. Was it visually interesting? Were they able to communicate their worth through design and words? Did they have an understanding of white space and professional documents? If they applied with a standard resume format without any type of personalization, they were not considered in the next round.

Graphic design jobs are not the only ones in which you should customize your resume design. Notice I said customize, not design – big difference. You want your resume to be somewhat standard, but include a flair that is uniquely you. If you add a different header font (make sure that it is legible), or a color sparingly, that can make a big impact. Your resume design speaks about who you are, so be critical about what customization tools you use and if it is appropriate for the company you are applying for. But above all else, make sure that your text and accomplishments are highlighted and easily formatted for online programs to scan.

And above all else, use a font size and style that are easy to read (no smaller than 10 point font and traditional font styles are preferred – my favorites are Arial Narrow, Tahoma and Garamond). White space is your friend – do not over-cram your information into one page. Instead, review your text and see if there are ways to make your accomplishments more concise.

Test how your resume looks to others. I am sure that you created a beautiful document… except when the recruiter views it, it is a hot mess. Make sure that you test your resume file in different browsers and opening modes. I tend to see the most mistakes with Word documents. The easiest solution, and preferred solution, is to always use a pdf document. The biggest blunders in Word have come courtesy of… opening it on a Mac, using Google docs to view, spacebar view (Mac), Windings font in Word. About 90% of the time, I will view the resume in a preview form – spacebar or Google Docs, to see if it is worth opening fully. Be sure that you see how your ressy's being seen, before you start applying.

The Easy Things

The easiest way to get your resume thrown out is with grammar errors. Seriously people, you want to show that you have some education and working knowledge of the English language. I know it is difficult to be a stickler about this as our everyday communications lack in this department, but this is an official document – treat it as such.

Check yourself for these things:

- Do not use "&" as a replacement for "and."
- Be careful/avoid contractions – I am a repeat offender with this. Make sure you review your resume several times hunting them out and replacing them (there's, I've, I'm, etc.).
- Be consistent in your punctuation choices. If you are using bullets, use the same type of bullets with the same indentation, each time. If you are ending a bullet with a period, make sure you end each bullet with a period. Get the point?
- In the body of your resume, use one consistent, easy-to-read font.
- Do not overuse stylization of font – bold, underline, italics. It makes your resume look confusing – use this sparingly and consistently throughout the document.
- Title your resume file with YOUR name – recruiters are looking at hundreds of resumes, it is incredibly difficult to remember who you are if you are one of 20 with a resume titled…resume. For you, it makes sense but please add your name so we can easily access it when we are ready to give you a call. My preference: LSmith_Resume.doc or Lisa_Smith_Resume.doc.
- Gmail is free – for the love of Nancy, please create a professional email account. Preferably an email that matches your actual name. I kid you not, I had someone with a three-name email address apply once – and when we spoke, she indicated that she had a new last name which didn't match anything in her resume or her email address. It was confusing and I never remembered to call her by the correct name.
- Read your resume out loud. Make sure that your grammar and sentence syntax flows smoothly and is not jarring at any one section. While you do not need to have perfect sentence structure, you need to avoid any awkward phrasing.

The Words You Choose

Each and every word that you choose for your resume should be considered carefully – not the point of analysis paralysis, but you should think through what you are saying and what your intent is. And then tweak again. I keep talking about "showing not telling" which is only accomplished through your word choice.

Use action words. Again, I repeat, use action words at every opportunity that you have. Your action words will support your accomplishments; explain what you did, how you did it and why it is important. And just in case you are not sure what action words are, I have included a list of them just for you.

So let us walk through some examples, shall we?

Example 1: "Work closely with multiple department managers and report monthly and quarterly results."

There are many things wrong with this example, but starting with the word choice, there are no action words – nothing makes me feel like I am witnessing something cool, with movement, a story – a beginning and an end. My critique would say this:

> What does work closely mean? Who are you working with? What kind of departments and what level are the managers? What types of reports? How are they generated? What type of impact do these reports have to the business? What value are you providing? How is this achievement outstanding?

Quite literally, what I am asking above in the critique is exactly what I said in my head when I saw this resume. I guarantee you that every recruiter is saying the same exact thing. The questions that I asked will help shape the action in the revised example.

Revised Example 1: "Established cross-divisional relationships with senior leadership to create and deliver monthly metrics and analysis through Xcelcius detailing sales efficiency rates."

Do you see the difference between the two examples? There is a ton of information and action packed into one bulleted resume sentence, but it shows me what actions you took (established, created, delivered), what you did (metrics and analysis), how you did it (using a difficult program, Xcelcius), and why I would care (you provided sales efficiency rates).

Example 2: "Conduct group and private lessons, 99% student pass rate."

My critique:

> Um, what kind of lessons were you providing, who was your target audience, what did you teach? Why is this significant and not just simply a part of your regular job duties? 99% seems high, but what is the normal pass rate? Why does this prove that you are a good teacher?"

Revised Example 2: "Created alternative learning methods for the school for Math and English, including group and private lessons available to students at no extra cost. Increased the pass rate from 72% to 99% within two years of taking over grade 5, having the highest pass rate in the district."

The action is clear (what was created), the target audience is identified (all students), innovation is shown (alternative, cost barrier). I now understand why the pass rate is significant and how *you* changed the status quo. All of these things help you stand out when considering candidates.

If you want an even bigger glimpse into my critique mind, I have several real examples and critiques available on the website (http://land-a-job.com).

And one last note about action words…be sure to use different action words throughout your resume. It makes me laugh when I see "managed" or "responsible for" at the beginning of every single bullet. Be creative, try and bring movement into your text. I sometimes think about a mystery novel and how each chapter has a cliffhanger – something that makes you want to continue to turn the page. Your resume should be the same thing – give the recruiter a reason to keep on reading.

Things You Should Already Know, But Forget Nonetheless

Here are a few more hints and tricks to help you along the way – I am sure that you knew these things at some point in time, but they have fallen off of your radar, so I am here to remind you. You will thank me later, I promise.

- Your location in your profile should match your resume, which would ideally, match the location of the job. If you are seeking a job in a different city or state, make sure you take the time to write a cover letter. Tell me why you are looking for a position in a different location – perhaps you are planning on moving to the area or you have family in the area. I do not really care WHY you are looking out-of-state, but in lieu of having a reason I am going to assume that you are simply applying for every single job that is posted. And if your profile location is different from your resume, it tells me that you are not at all detail-oriented and not taking time to update your resume for each submission. Get it? Pay attention to all of the details.
- I can track you – ok, maybe not stalker-esque, but recruiters can see all of the positions that you have applied to at their company. When you apply to everything that the company has open, or two very different jobs, you are not going to be high-up on either list. It is confusing – do you want to do marketing or sales? IT or HR? You are not an expert at everything, so please only apply to the ONE job that you

really want. If it is a larger company, be sure to stick within similar job descriptions/titles/departments. You not only lose your credibility by applying to everything, you also look lazy and desperate.

- Do not lie on resume, ever. Nuff said.

Cover Letters

Ugh, I was hoping to avoid a section on cover letters, so I left it for the very end of the resume section. I loathe cover letters like most of you, but it is a necessary evil in today's application process. To be honest, I am a repeat offender of the "always use a stellar cover letter" advice. Although, in my defense, I have not applied for a job in today's environment, so I think I can be forgiven. But given today's environment with so many qualified candidates searching and applying for the same job – your cover letter can speak volumes about why you are the most qualified. It should highlight your qualifications, show a bit of your personality and share teasers or hooks to engage the hiring manager to read more. I know, it is a lot to fit into a small package.

Why do I hate cover letters? As a recruiter, it is one more thing that I have to read, make a decision about, and then keep/file. They are usually so manufactured and standardized that there is little to be gained from them. They can induce ridiculous errors that do nothing but annoy me – not using my name, calling me sir, having the wrong company name in the letter, including a different position, and so on. If you are not planning on customizing your cover letter, just leave it off altogether (but remember – you may immediately be thrown into the "no" pile since everyone else has included one).

Things to remember about your cover letter:

1. **The cover letter goes in the body of your email**. I am not sure how or why so many people get this wrong, but do not attach your cover letter… anywhere. When you apply via email, your email IS your cover letter – so put all of the

goodies in the actual body of the email. When you are applying via online program, I recommend pasting your cover letter into the given space, versus doing it as an upload. This way, you know exactly which cover letter you have attached and it helps alleviate another blunder. The recruiter is not going to waste time opening another document, so make it as easy as possible for them to get a snapshot of what you bring to the table.

2. Have **three simple and short paragraphs** – that is it.
    - Paragraph one: tell me who you are, where you found the position, which position you are applying for, and one engaging fact.
    - Paragraph two: your differentiators – what makes you the best candidate for the job and what skills and/or experience do you have that directly relates to my position that is not highlighted verbatim on your resume.
    - Paragraph three: leave me with one fun or interesting nugget to remember you and also how and when you can be contacted.

3. **Do not say "I'm the best candidate for this job."** I am already assuming you feel you are the best candidate for the job since you applied for the job. Instead, SHOW me all of the ways you are the best fit. What have you done that would support that statement, what else? Keep digging deeper until you are sure that your dad (or insert another non-industry adult) would understand your accomplishments, without knowing you personally.

4. **Leave all of the BS (bull$h*t) off.** There is nothing worse than coming across as a fake, phony, or conceited in a cover letter – and trust me, a recruiter can spot it a mile away. Your tone should be professional, concise, and to the point. And above all else, it should be fact. Your cover letter (or any job-seeking materials) should be rooted in fact, not smoke and

mirrors. If you include items in your resume that seem too good to be true (I am the best at Sales, better at Research and Development, and top-achiever in Marketing), you will be overlooked – even if it is true. So be consistent about your cover letter topic so it does not sound like BS.

5. **We only really read these when we are on the fence about you**. This is your supporting material and is your only opportunity besides your resume to gain my interest. Your tone should be confident, your personality should shine through, and you should absolutely show off your experience and assets. This is your own personal back-up collateral, so make sure it represents you in your best light.

6. **Remove the gimmicks, insults, and superlatives**. If you are making me roll my eyes, you are going in the no pile. I do not want to hear what your colleagues say about you, or how great your parents think you are. I want to see actual results – "I launched two HR departments at small companies which resulted in X, Y, and Z. This experience will directly correlate with the change management initiative responsibilities you've included in the job description."

7. **Your cover letter should be specific to each position.** While I also believe in tweaking your resume for each application (if applicable), updating your cover letter for each application is a must. There is no excuse for you not to include only relevant information here – address the hiring manager properly if you are applying directly, include the company name and the correct position title, and be sure that you address specific accomplishments from the required skills.

8. **No one cares about the classes you took and other miscellaneous information.** Being a new grad is ok – hiring managers have all been there. But when you list "relevant coursework" in your cover letter, or even worse – on your resume, you look like a moron. Everyone knows that real life

experience vastly differs from anything you have learned in a classroom. You are wasting valuable space in your cover letter when discussing "I got an 'A' in Accounting," or "I may not have real life experience, but I took many business courses in college." These facts may help you when on the job, but it is more important for you to SHOW how you utilize the skills you have learned.

9. **Show, not tell** (is this sinking in yet?).This takes practice and is not natural for many people. But your cover letter should show the hiring manager how you have accomplished things and a well-rounded look at your experience. Do not tell me that you did something, tell me what makes it special that you did it. For example:

    - Tell: I was the top salesman at the company.
    - Show: I was ranked 1 across the 33 sales people at the company, increasing profits over 13% which equated to $30,000 of new business.
    - See the difference? The "Tell" does not provide me with a reference point. I am left asking… so what? When you show me, I am able to see the significance of your achievement.

10. **Have some personality**. A boring form letter will not cut it anymore. Let your unique voice shine through. Your cover letter should be written in first person (no references like "Anzman does" or "Melissa can") and should come across as though you are in an interview – condensed into three short paragraphs. Boring is easily overlooked but obnoxious will not win you any friends either. Be YOU, write about YOU, SHOW the hiring manager what YOU bring to the table and you will have instant cover letter personality.

Chapter 5 – The Search and Apply

* * *

Unfortunately the perfect job is not going to come and knock at your door while you are sitting on your couch – but wouldn't that be dreamy? You have to go out there and find your next job and it takes work. And here is a key nugget to remember throughout the search and apply process: **it is not personal**. I know, it is so hard to really believe that because after all, this is *your* career and job hunt we are talking about, but not being called for an interview is not reflective of who you are as person, it is indicative that you are not a good fit, for whatever reason, for the position for which you applied. Instead, think about what advice you would give your best friend if they were bummed about not being called – "don't worry about it, there is nothing more you could have done, you are not the problem." Now, heed your own advice!

Numbers Game

The more jobs you are qualified to fill to which you apply, the higher the chances are that you will land the job of your dreams. There is not a magic number that leads to the right job, but I do know that you up your chances of getting a phone interview with each application. One of the most frustrating things I hear when working with friends and clients about their job search is that they applied for five jobs and have not yet heard anything back. Applying for one to five jobs a week, is not considered a job hunt. When I am personally going through the job hunt process, I spend about two hours a day, usually late at night, hunting for the best jobs to apply for and apply for as many as I can in that time period, around ten or so, every single day. And guess what – I get call backs all of the time. When you have a strong resume and you are putting yourself out there so that the odds are in your favor, you *will* start getting calls.

One of my friends is notorious for ignoring the "numbers game" rule. She stops herself from applying for jobs because she:

- "Thinks it is an awesome job, but she's not sure if she is qualified enough for it."
- "Is not sure if her resume materials match the quality level for the awesome job."
- "Lacks the self-confidence to go after the job because she doesn't want the hiring manager to laugh at her for thinking she could do this job."

I am sure she has many other excuses that prevent her from playing the numbers game, but the reasons above are ridiculous (sorry). If you are interested in the job and/or even if you simply want interview practice, you get NO WHERE without applying for the damn job. Plain and simple. No one is searching for you to fill their position – you must throw your hat in the ring. If your resume materials are not up to par, then you are clearly stalling. You have all of the tools from the previous sections to create a stellar package, so move past the tactical barrier and get it done.

And the last one is the one that I want to somewhat giggle at, although many people feel the same way. I think this fear comes from worrying what other people think about you, from your high school days. But here is the reality – a) if you are applying through an online application system, then the recruiter will not even see your resume if it is well outside the bounds of what they are looking for; b) the recruiter has ZERO time to pass judgment on you or your resume other than "yes, I'll contact her" or "no, thank you." Regardless, you absolutely must get over your own internal barriers and start hitting "apply" – you never know what the hiring manager is looking for and you could have talked yourself out of a fantastic opportunity, simply by worrying about being a perfect fit.

Where to Find the Jobs

There are so many websites where you can find job postings. I hate to admit this, but there was a time in my career, early on I should point out, that I had to use the newspaper to find job openings. In fact, one of my jobs was 100% centered around entering employment ads into different newspapers. Go ahead and chuckle at my age, but it was almost easier to find jobs that way – you knew exactly where to look to find qualified jobs. Today, with the plethora of sites out there including individual company job sites, the landscape is a bit more difficult to navigate. Regardless of the resources you decide to use, it is important to not get hung up on only one site. There are options out there for a reason, and different jobs can be found in different online locations.

SimplyHired.com

SimplyHired is my favorite job search site. I have used it for many years and have been very pleased to see how it has grown and perfected the aggregate job site concept. It is the place where I always start my job hunt and my clients have had the most success from this site, as well. Essentially, SimplyHired aggregates open positions across the globe from other job boards and company sites, and puts them in one place for you. So instead of having to go to each company you are interested in, doing a search to see if they have an open position in your field in a specific location, SimplyHired brings all of that information to you with one search.

The site is a huge resource, although there are a few things to beware of. First, the narrowing process is a bit off – if you search for a specific job title versus years of experience, you may be missing out on opportunities. I combat this by doing a more general search (example 1 below) and then using the years of experience function or weed through what pops up (example 2 below). The other thing to be aware of is that while it aggregates *many* jobs, it does not encompass *every* open job. Its software works well with big companies who use the well-known online application programs, but it can easily miss smaller company job postings.

Example 1:

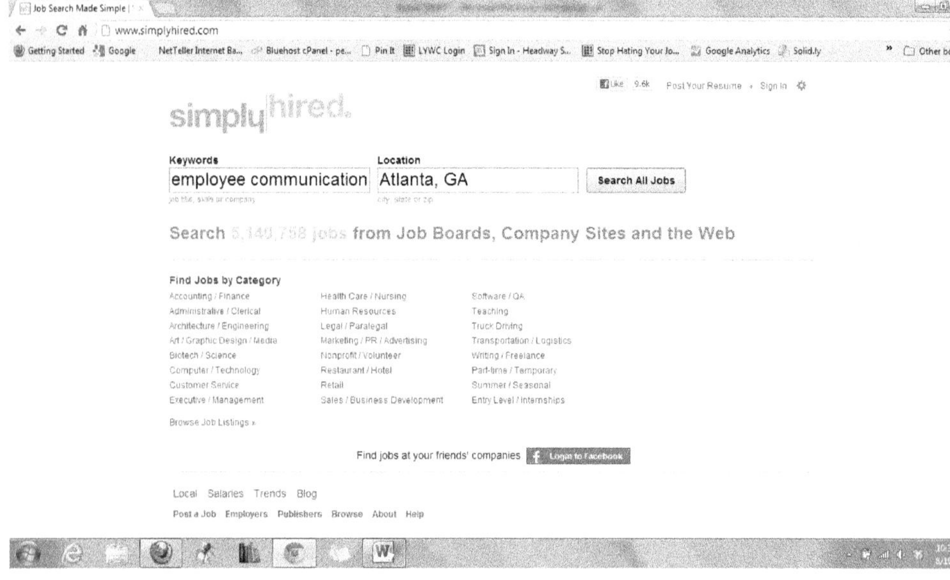

Example 2:

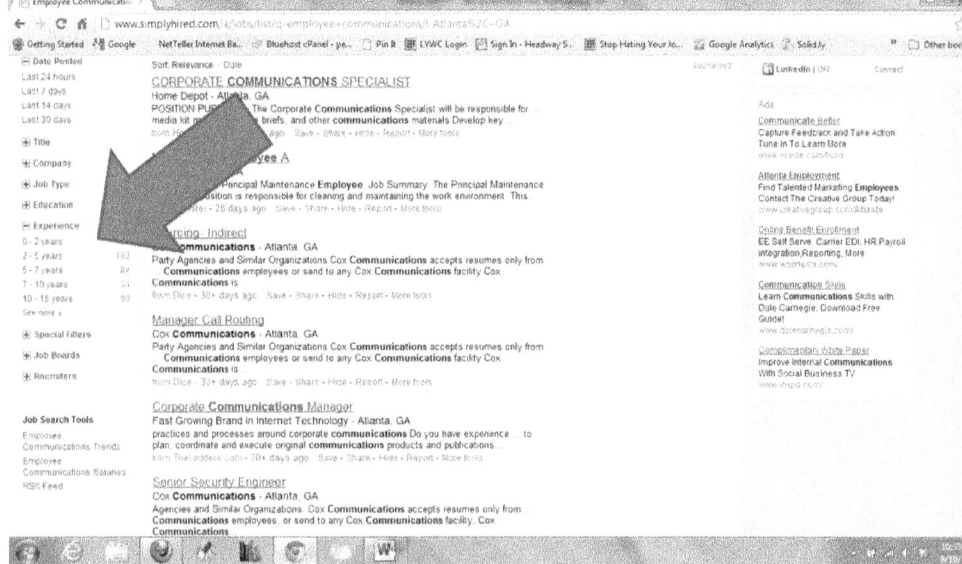

LinkedIn Jobs

LinkedIn (LI) is one of the best job boards out there in my opinion. It is easy for all companies, big and small, to post on the site (cost of posting is reasonable) and the hiring manager has the opportunity to interact directly with the candidates. It provides a somewhat real-time matching process where the recruiter can find out significant information about the interested candidate instantly. LI is somewhat new to the job board game as it was an extension of their overall brand that has grown steadily and significantly over the years. For jobs that have historically been considered "white collar," this is a key place to include in your job hunt.

Remember from Chapter 2, the recruiter can see *everything* about you when you apply, so make sure it is all up to par. In addition, postings tend to go in cycles – tons of applicants on day one and then it slows down significantly. So strategize appropriately – there will be an overwhelming number of applicants the first day a job is posted. The flip side of that coin is they may strike gold on the first day and no longer need to keep fielding applicants. Conundrum, no? From being on the other end, here is what I would advise: stay away from applying on the very first day and submit your application on day two or three (ideally). It is extremely difficult to keep up with the incoming emails and resumes on day one, and the recruiter is going to have to wait until the inbox dings settle down before weeding through the mess. After the first week, review the number of candidates that have applied before applying – if the number is low, as in fewer than 150, then apply. Otherwise, they are probably weeding through candidates already and your resume could be lost in the shuffle.

FlexJobs.com

Oh how I love the promise and potential of this job board. The concept is simple – they do the grunt work to find part-time, freelance, and telecommuting positions at *real* companies across the U.S., and then provide them to you… for a small fee. I am always torn about paying money to find open jobs, BUT in this case, if you are seeking a non-traditional position, then this could be a great solution for you. And they let you try it before you buy it – you can do a quick job search to see if there are any potential positions that meet your criteria, but you will need a subscription to get the application details. One thing to be aware of is that a few of their job postings are indicated as “telecommute,” but when you explore further on the employer’s site, it says that “telecommuting is a possibility.” That is not something that occurs often and is by no means the fault of FlexJobs, but it is something you should explore for each application.

These types of jobs are difficult to find, especially as so many of these jobs are posted on traditional job boards and end up being scams or work from home infomercials. If you are ready to make the plunge into a different type of job path, then definitely check out this site and evaluate the potential bang for your buck, before purchasing.

Monster.com and CareerBuilder.com

I am asked all of the time if I think Monster and CareerBuilder are the best places to search for a job. I think they were five to ten years ago, but not a great place for you to start today. Remember, these sites were trailblazers when they were created and have struggled with changing to compete better. Both are very expensive for employers to use for a job posting and their application feed is overwhelming for recruiters. Because of this, most recruiters will not accept or even look at applications through these job boards.

Even with the downside, these sites do excel in a few things. They are a great place to search for entry-level positions across industries and allow you to post your resume for all to find. They are also still the main stomping ground for what is called “Resume Mining.” This means that recruiters go to these job boards and search for qualified candidates for their open positions using your posted resume as their search material. If you are open to having conversations with headhunters or external recruiters, or are looking to get your foot in the door in a different industry, than posting your resume on these sites can be beneficial to you. And know that aggregate sites like

SimplyHired will capture the postings from both Monster and CareerBuilder, so doing a separate search on these sites is redundant (not to mention frustrating, usually).

TheLadders.com

The premise for TheLadders was quite "revolutionary" when they first launched. They charge the job seekers for them to gain access to six-figure job postings. Some job postings are exclusively listed and others are posted elsewhere on the web. They also have different "ladders" for specific skillsets including Marketing, Sales and Human Resources. The site also provides resume critiques and recruiter connections that you can seek out, turning the script around when it comes to "resume mining."

I have used TheLadders before as a job hunter, but I am hard-pressed to recommend you using it in the current landscape. I do not believe that you *need* to pay to see open positions. It is the lazy way to find good jobs. But when the jobs are posted elsewhere for you to find easily with a simple search, I struggle to find the real value with this site. Here is what I would recommend, particularly if you are seeking (and qualified for, of course), a six-figure position that is a senior manager level or above, try out their basic service. It is free to try – you will only see job titles, but you will get a sense of what types of positions they have available and if you think it is worth your money to invest in the hunt (that is a personal decision). If you skip TheLadders, you will not be missing out on anything, but if this concept interests you, take it for a test spin.

Going Local

If commute concerns are high up on your list for potential positions or perhaps you want to aim to land a job at a smaller business, the best way to do that is to go local and pound the pavement. Not in the traditional sense; I am not advising that you go door to door to hand out your resumes, but a local approach.

Approach 1: Do some online research on your desired target area's better business bureau and chamber of commerce's websites. Most of them provide a list of local businesses in the area with additional information about each one – what kind of business they are, how long they have been in their location, and so on. From this list, start going to the company's websites that you are interested in learning more about and search for positions on their site.

Approach 2: This approach will deliver even greater results, but it does take some effort on your behalf. Essentially: get in your car! You will be absolutely amazed when you drive around an office park or even around your town/city, and see how many businesses are really there. I tend to start at a business park and get out of my car to explore. If there are signs posted outside with company names that is a good start. But even better is if you go into the lobby and take notes on the list of businesses in the directory. (Warning – for buildings in New York City, this may be a bit more difficult, but most places across the U.S. do not have building entry security, so this should be an option). From that list, research the companies, see which ones interest you, and apply for positions.

Approach 3: Networking is always a great way to find out about new opportunities and connecting with the right people. Join a local networking group and add value each meeting. This is a *slow* process, but will set you up for local success further down the road.

Applicant Tracking Systems

Our hiring process is absolutely flawed, I agree with you. Hiring managers and recruiters cannot possibly connect with each and every candidate for each and every job to find out if you are better "in person" than on your resume. Instead, many companies use an applicant tracking system (ATS) which allows candidates to submit their resume and supporting materials online. If you have applied for a job in the past five years, you are probably familiar with them. These are the sites where you have to log-in and create a registration name to apply and then you can select jobs to put in your basket or cart to save for later or apply to. It stores your resume materials for you and makes it the most painful process as possible when you first sign-up, but then it is a cinch to keep applying at that same company. Know what I am talking about?

There are many different types of ATSs, and the newer ones are a lot more user- and candidate- friendly, but they are essentially all screening systems so that time is not wasted on clearly under-qualified candidates. There are humans on the other side of the ATS as well, but the first screen is done through a powerful scanning system that matches your application input and the words from your resume to the job qualifications for each specific position. Once you have been deciphered by the ATS, your information will either be sent to the "no" pile, or will be emailed to the recruiter for the position. The email the recruiter receives usually includes your application information highlights in the body of the email with your resume as an attachment or in a "view separately" format. Why am I telling you this? So you understand what the guidance I am about to give…

You must complete the most important sections in the ATS. Some people tend to skip over entering their relevant experience in the application portion and rely on their resume alone to land them an interview. Same with entering your education or even answering some of the basic questions the company asks. This information is what is the most easily accessible to recruiters – it is **in the body** of their notification email. It is what will sell you as a candidate to get them to open your attached resume. Getting the picture here? As annoying as it is to enter all of your information into the ATS for each company, it is necessary. I have written a lot about how to hack ATS's from a "make it easier please" perspective, so be sure to check out my Online Application Guide.

And my last word about ATS's, here is a step-by-step guide to make your life easier when you are ready to start applying.

1. If you are seeking a position in another state or city and you have plans to relocate to that area (as in, you are going to pay for it on your own), I would advise selecting the city/location

where the position is, in the drop-down menu. If the position does not have relocation indicated, then selecting a different location will most likely put you in the "no" pile.

2. Enter enough information that the system believes you to be qualified for the job, but do not waste your time on "information gathering" questions. For example, in the "Preferences section": select highest education level, job level and job type, but skip shift preference and employee status. What about salary requirements? I would recommend skipping this question if it is optional. It gives you a bit more wiggle room and also will help you not be screened out for being in a range too high or too low than expected for the position.

3. Having everything saved in a Word document is quite handy when you get to the "Experience" section. This is typically an abbreviated version of your previous roles, in addition to your resume. Be sure to review this section for each position, as there are usually errors when it is pulled from your resume. How many previous positions do you need to include? It depends on how much experience you have and what you are trying to show (and how much information the company is asking for). If you have been in the workforce for many years (15+), there is no need to enter all 10 jobs you have had. **Just be sure to include the most relevant positions and the past three**, at a minimum. New or recent grads, a little advice – be smart about which positions you include. Internships are great if they were truly internships, but do not include resume fluff positions as they will not help add value to your overall package consideration.

4. Have the following information ready: your previous supervisor(s) name, title, phone number; and start/end dates. For positions that require a security clearance or bonding (and even some companies with government contracts), you will need even more detailed information. Have the previous addresses and dates of residence for the previous 7 – 10 years

handy. I keep this information as a contact item in my email contact list, as I learned the hard way, there is no good way to remember this all. Oh, and that includes all of your college residences as well if it falls within that time frame.

How to Increase Your Odds

All this talk about it being a numbers game is a good start, but if you are not approaching it cohesively, you will feel as though you are a falling tree in the forest. It *is* a numbers game, but you can absolutely increase your odds of landing an awesome job if you take the time and effort.

Networking

I cannot stress enough how crucial networking is to your overall career success. And this is coming from someone who loathes networking. But who you know is so important when you are looking for a job regardless of the type of job. When you are "networking," you want to make a real effort to get to know the person you are meeting and adding value as much as possible in the conversation.

Meeting someone a few times does not make a strong connection – especially if you are trying to sell them on hiring you each time you see them. Instead, networking is about making a lasting impression and cultivating a relationship with the other person. The only way I am able to get through networking events is by believing that I am at the event to *make new friends*. Not connections, not people who will submit my resume for me, but extending my circle of people I know and like.

Who You Know

When you are on the job hunt, you need to rely upon the people around you to help funnel leads your way. But there is a very fine line between help and annoying your contacts. You should avoid sending a mass email to everyone letting them know you are job hunting. Personal touch is key here – and nothing says "I am lazy" more than a mass email asking for this kind of help. Send individualized emails letting them know what you are up to and *ask for their help*. Be sure to be specific in your request, as in the exact position you are seeking, and attach your resume to your email.

Approach people with class and be concise. I receive these types of emails all of the time, part of the benefit and curse of being in HR, and here are some examples that made me want to pull my hair out:

- *"I am looking for a job, can you help me?"* Um, that was the entire email.
- *"I saw this open position and I know we talked at length that the company was awful, but will you hook me up with that position anyway?"* Why in the world would I be helping you get a job that I know will not work out? Especially if we have previously discussed the job or company at length, this request deserves a face palm. No, I will not help you do that – I refuse to help you into a bad situation, even if you are that desperate.
- *"I was just fired and am looking for a job. Do you know of anyone who is hiring?"* Throwing the "fired" word out there makes me concerned, especially without any additional details. If you want to include that kind of information, provide some context about why (laid off, budget cuts, etc).
- *"I really need to get out of this job that I'm in. Although I love it and have been here for 20 years, the projected work does not look good. I can't keep going through this year after year. I'll be 46 this year, and I'm thinking I need to make a change now - not when I'm 50+ and no one wants to hire me. Can you help point me in the right direction?"* I had to long-quote this doozy since there were so many areas of concern. 1) The fact that you are concentrating on your age concerns me. 2) What direction would you like me to point you in? Getting your resume materials together? How to apply?

> Connecting you with leads? I am clueless as to *how* I can help you. 3) What type of position are you looking for?

Absolutely pool your team to help you, but they should not be doing the legwork for you. It is still up to you to lead them to the water and make it easy for them to drink.

Qualified Applications

I discussed this earlier, but your chances of landing a great job increase in relation to how qualified you are for each position you apply to. It is obviously more difficult to land jobs that are at the next level or stretch jobs, so level-set your application ratio standards when considering titles to apply for. And as a reminder: just because you believe you are qualified to do a job, you are not qualified for it if you do not meet the minimum requirements from the job description.

Tying it All Together

Nothing matters if you do not have your sh*t together. Your resume materials must be stellar, should present you in the amazing light that you deserve, and need to specific. Update them for each job description to take advantage of ATS programs and consistently prove why you are the best candidate for the job.

Being **persistent** is a critical component to your success with getting hired. You cannot take rejection personally or use it as an excuse to give up completely. The last person standing is the one who wins – so keep at it regardless of the bumps along the way. Your persistence will pay off for you in ways you never could imagine: you will have a job, you will have made new connections, and you will have stepped out of your comfort zone.

How I Landed My Jobs

This is a bit embarrassing to write about, but I get this question all of the time: "how did you land all of your great jobs?" So I am opening the vault of my many, many job-hunting-to-offer experiences to shed some light on the process as well as show you that I have snagged jobs through different channels.

Job 1: Account Coordinator at a jewelry manufacturer (Long Island City, NY)

Through a family friend. I decided to move to New York City without a job and right after 9/11. I know, not the wisest choice. But I did have a job lead from a family friend whose sister was working at a jewelry manufacturer. He gave me her cell number and when I arrived in NYC I called her the next day to see if they had any open positions. She set-up a meeting for me to meet with the owner the following day. He hired me on the spot and I started the following week in a job I never knew existed. Did you know real, live people string every necklace that is sold at Macy's, etc. and that they are HAND price-tagged? And that is how I officially began my adult career.

Job 2: Account Coordinator at a recruitment advertising agency (New York, NY)

Cold resume submission (snail-mail). My dream was to work in advertising, so I was set to make it happen (jewelry was not really my thing). I was mailing out about five resumes a week as I was not urgently seeking a new position, but wanted to keep my pulse on the market. From a cold resume mailing, I received a call to interview with hiring manager (the account manager) and meet the division head. After my onsite interview, I was offered the position the following day.

Job 3: Publicity and Marketing Coordinator at a book publishing company (New York, NY)

Employee referral. Talk about dream job? OMG – I am an avid reader and was a wanna-be writer, so this was a dream job I could not even dream. But when I started noticing several people being laid off from the advertising job, I knew that I had to find something else to jump-to urgently. So I asked my friends if they knew of anything and one of my new friends was working at the publishing company at the time. She said that there were a few positions open and that she would be happy to put my resume forward as an employee referral. Being a referral, my resume was actually looked at and I made it past the two rounds of interviews to land a pretty cool job.

Job 4: Senior Publicist at a major magazine (New York, NY)

Connection and proven work history with hiring manager. Part of my job at the book publishing company was working closely with authors and their external publicity agencies. One of my authors, Jason Zweig, was ramping up to promote an updated version of *The Intelligent Investor.* While working with him, he introduced me to his external publicist and we worked together well. When she had a need to fill in a position during a maternity leave, she offered it to me – with some strings. First, I would be freelance, getting paid hourly and responsible for my own health insurance. Second, the position would only last during the maternity leave, so a three month contract. I scooped it up and worked hard – jumping out on my own for the first time.

Job 5: HR and Employee Communications Manager at a luxury brand magazine publisher (New York, NY)

Connection through a direct report. I had an intern while I was at the magazine company and we got along great – he was smart, a quick learner and fun to work with. What I did not know was that he was also the son of a very important person. He introduced me to his dad (I was still clueless as to who he was) and talked up my skillset and my ending contract. His dad created a position for me that he had been pondering for some time and hired me to launch the department. This is still the coolest story in my arsenal.

Job 6: Business HR and HR Communications Manager at a medical device company (San Diego, CA)

Direct hire through their online career section. I was new to the area and did not have any leads or connections, so I applied to as many jobs in the areas as possible. I ended up getting two offers on the same day with this job, both leads through the same channel. Anyway, I found this position through SimplyHired and applied directly on the company's website, noting that the position was due to close the following day. Within one hour of applying, I received a call from the recruiter and set up my interview.

Job 7: Director of HR at a small promotions business (Atlanta, GA)

Direct hire through LinkedIn. I was applying to specific jobs that met my bridge job qualifications and found this one on LinkedIn. I applied to it directly and received a call back from the owner for an interview. I received another offer close to this one as well, and that position was through applying on the company's online application site.

There are several freelance gigs, extended offers and part-time jobs that I have not included above since they are not as relevant to you. But hopefully my splendid seven examples show you just how many ways one person can land a job through leveraging the numbers game and exploring different channels.

Chapter 6 – Interviewing

* * *

So your fantastic networking skills and your resume have landed you an interview – amazing! Now is the hard part, so to speak – this is where it can easily go so wrong. Knowing how to interview well will absolutely set you apart from the other candidates and get you hired. If you are not a super star interviewee, your search will be significantly longer and more painful. So let's turn you into the best interviewee of all time!

There are a few overarching concepts that will help you throughout any interview:

1. **This *is* a popularity contest of sorts**. How you engage the people who are interviewing you, does matter. Come across as affable, intelligent, and easy to work with, you will be hired. Think about this before you answer.
2. Even in casual work environments, people take the interview process seriously. So how you present yourself, **how *professionally* you present yourself, is important**. Do not be fooled by the "we wear jeans" culture – that is fine when you have the job, but until then, dress up.
3. The more **STARs you can use to answer each question**, the better off you are (more on this later).

Oh, and do not forget that *you* are supposed to be interviewing the company as well. During the interview process, make sure you learn as much as you can about the hierarchy structure and title system; general company information and values; company culture; and the turn over and retention rates. Be sure to review these items along the way and learn more about them in Chapter 6.

The Interview Process

Every company is different, but the general flow for interviewing candidates is roughly the same across various industries. Your first interview in the process will be a phone screen. Essentially these are 30 – 60 minutes in length, where you will speak with the recruiter. They are talking with you to screen you in or out – and you would be surprised at just how many people never make it past the initial phone interview (more on this later). During the phone screen, your overall experience will be discussed and so will your communication skills. If you are a good match for what the hiring manager has asked the recruiter to find, then you will be sent to the next round.

The next round of interviews can either be onsite or via phone and will be with the hiring manager (the person who will be your boss). The larger the company, the more likely it will be via phone. The hiring manager will try and get a sense of your background, but more importantly, if your personality would fit on his/her team and within the culture of the company and if he/she thinks they can manage you. Not very objective, but such is the reality of this process.

The next round will be onsite interviews. You will meet with the hiring manager and if they are good at recruiting, you will meet with other members of the team. They may do these onsite interviews at once, which is the best practice, or in several different onsite meetings. Either way, these interviews will be the most formal of the process and will be the deciding factor for your candidacy. So that is the overall process… in a nutshell.

Once you have applied, your job is to keep hunting for new jobs. **DO NOT call the recruiter to see if they received your application** (big pet peeve people!). They are digging through hundreds of resumes at once for each position, with several positions open at the same time. If they are interested, if you meet the qualifications, if you forgot to attach your resume and they think you may be a fit, and so on, they will reach out to you. Email works. They got your application. By calling them (ahem, and interrupting their resume search), guess what – you have moved yourself over to the "no" pile. Recruiters do not need to hear from you personally to ensure that they a) have received your resume; b) remember you; c) hear you explain why you are qualified for the position. If you are the best person for the job, if you are the most qualified person for the job, include that information ON YOU RESUME. Put the phone down!

And one quick side-note about salary conversations: you should have the conversation with the recruiter OR the first person who asks you. Keep the discussion consistent with one person, without any backroom negotiations by trying to talk more out of a different interviewee – this is a big no-no and can easily get you dropped out of the running.

Know thy Recruiter

The most important thing to remember when interacting with a recruiter for the first time is that the easiest way to his/her heart is to **make life easier for them**. They have probably spent the past week or longer doing nothing but looking at hundreds, if not thousands of resumes, fielding questions and demands from the hiring manager, and are annoyed by all of the follow-up phone calls they are receiving from candidates who do not have a chance in hell to land the job. In other words, they are annoyed, frazzled, and ready to move this position from "sourcing" status to "hired" status. And YOU are the person to make that happen.

If your resume was the first glimpse the recruiter had of you and who you are, your response to an interview request is the second opportunity you have, to make a strong first impression. They already like you or you would not have been asked to continue in the process, so remove all of the doubt and know that you *are* qualified for the job and a viable candidate.

Recruiters are busy – they are usually working on several (think: 10 – 30) open positions at any given time, and the last thing they want to do is manage scheduling interviews and what not (luckily, most have assistants or coordinators do this for them). That being said, you should assume that all of your communication with the Recruiting department, will be kept on file and part of your overall candidate assessment. Got it?

In addition to making their life amazing, it is so important that you kill them with kindness and professionalism. I cannot stress this enough. Some people treat recruiters as necessary evils, or "the help." If you are one of those people, I can guarantee you that you will not be landing a job anytime soon. Recruiters are a huge part of the hiring process and have a say in the process – in fact, they are your gatekeepers. Piss them off, you will not even get a chance. Be kind, respect their time, and help them do their job better.

Setting-up the Interview

Ding – your inbox just beeped letting you know that you *finally* have caught the attention of a recruiter! Excitement, delight and perhaps relief are going through your mind. Take a moment to do a mini-celebration, and then put your game face back on. Now is not the time to slack – it is time to bring your "A game" and start responding!

Be Available

When you receive an availability request, be available. One thing that constantly annoys me when I am recruiting, are any of the following responses to my phone interview request (stated as follows: "Hi Joe, I'd like to set up a 30 minute phone interview with you. Will you please let me know what your availability looks like over the next several days so we can get something scheduled?")

- Response 1: I'm wide open, just let me know what works for you
- Response 2: 10:30am tomorrow works for me

With response one, not only do you come across as somewhat desperate to find a job even though your intent was to be accommodating, but you also have now necessitated an additional email exchange with me checking a date/time back with you. Remember the other candidates the recruiter is trying to interview? Yeah – recruiters do not need any additional emails, promise. Response two only provides me with one option, leaving me to think A) you are unable to follow simple instructions/requests, so I am wondering if you just did not pay attention; B) you do not want a new job; C) perhaps you are a bit self-centered, thinking that you are the only one with a busy schedule. Um, none of these three things are the first impression you want to leave. And I will **share a little secret** – if the candidate pool is very strong, there have been times with I have simply removed the above "annoying" candidate out of the potential pool and into the "no" pile.

Hopefully you get it – so instead of being too broad or too narrow in your availability, here is what I am looking for:

> "Hi Recruiter, I'm excited for the opportunity to meet with you via phone about the position. Here's my availability, please let me know if you'd like additional dates/times, or feel free to schedule during any of the available time slots below, and I can be reached at 404-867-5309. I'm free: Monday, 9 – 1 1am, after 2pm; Tuesday, 12 – 3 pm; or Wednesday, 9 – 11 am. I look forward to connecting with you."

You have been very clear about when you are free and will work your availability into my schedule. Then all I have to do is simply email you back my preferred date and time, and viola – we are confirmed!

Be Concise

It should not be a surprise that conciseness is important in this phase of the interview process. Do not try to add additional selling points or supporting material to your interview request response. In most cases an assistant will be doing the dirty work anyway, so your efforts will be wasted on someone who is completely out of the loop.

But more than that, there is no need for the additional information clutter. You can attack them with more insight and accomplishments when you actually speak with the recruiter, you have already convinced them that you warrant that discussion, so do not blow it by being too eager or too verbose.

Stand Out Like a STAR

How do you really stand out above the rest? By leveraging the HR tools available to you. To be honest, I had not encountered these hidden jewels until I was *firmly* on the inside of HR – in other words, several years in. I have no idea why, but for some reason, actual interview techniques are a guarded secret. Until now, of course.

Behavioral Interviewing

While there is not a proven method of "good" interviewing and every recruiter/company has their own "best practices," simply asking about what you did each day or gauging your personality, does not indicate any type of future success in a role. Because of these outdated interview approaches, many of the top companies have changed their process and focus on, or intersperse their interviews, with behavioral-based questioning.

This is exactly what it sounds like – what behaviors and actions did you take in previous roles that could indicate success or failure in the position you are applying for? They are seeking out specific examples of what you did and how you did it.

And the best part is that even if recruiters are not transparent with you about using this technique, you should still answer as many interview questions as possible in this format! The easiest way to do this is by thinking like a STAR. STAR stands for:

- Situation/Task
- Action
- Result

In each response, you should cover all parts of the STAR in your example. So if you were asked:
Describe a new procedure or idea you conceived within the past year. Your STAR response would be:

- **Situation/Task**: I created a new performance management system that integrated employee performance with not only specific job expectations, but also with the company's core values.
- **Action:** By evaluating the previous system and interviewing employees and managers, I was able to determine the inherent biases and remove the rampant subjectivity in reviewing employees.
- **Result:** The company now has a standardized performance management system across the company and is able to reward behaviors based on their core values.

STAR's should be considered your best friend – the more STAR examples you are able to provide, the stronger your candidacy. This structure allows you to explain what you did, how you did it, and why it is significant, all in a concise manner. From a recruiter or hiring manager's perspective, you will come across as a strong candidate by showing your accomplishments and also by not wasting their time in your delivery. It's a win-win for all – it just takes practice.

So before you begin the interview process, make sure you have answered the following questions in full (for each position type). I have provided a worksheet to keep in front of you, here. I promise this exercise will have the biggest bang for your buck. Seriously, do not skip this!

Five Sample Behavioral Questions:

1. Tell me about one of the toughest groups you've had to work with. What was the situation? What did you do? How did it turn out?

2. What do you do to keep informed about changes in your organization/business/strategy? What was the impact of your actions?

3. Describe a time when you improved the productivity/profitability of your work unit. How did you identify these opportunities for improvement?

4. Tell me about a time you were involved in a project that ran into problems? What did you do?

5. Sometimes strict organizational policies make it very difficult to get our work done. Can you think of a time when you had to bend a rule to get your work done more efficiently?

Want more? No worries, I have you covered. I have shared every single behavioral question I have EVER used during the interview process as part of the bonus package. Be sure to check them out on the website (http://land-a-job.com).

Master the Phone Interview

The phone interview is a critical piece in the hiring process, and one that many people overlook because it does not have the glitz, glamour and necessary attire, as an in-person interview. However, this *is* the gatekeeper call – in order to even have a chance of meeting the hiring manager, you have to ace this part of the process.

Be Reachable

Make sure that you are reachable via a reliable connection. Cell phones are usually reliable connections these days, but they are definitely NOT fail-proof. I have been on the recruiting side of interviews where the cell phone dropped the call because they were apparently in a poor coverage area. Here is the thing, I know that you are not responsible for technology malfunctioning, but the bottom line is, you have wasted my time when your phone drops and we have to try and track each other down again – bad first impression. Here are the biggest no-no's:

- Do not schedule a phone interview when you are going to be driving in the car. Period. I do not care if you have a hands-free device, you are not giving me your full attention, so I am not inclined to give you mine. In addition, I do not want to hear a car wreck over the phone (it has happened before which is why I have a zero-tolerance policy on this).
- Make sure you have a quiet place to have the call – being outside in the wind does not count.
- Remove any ring-back music from your cell line. Honestly, people.
- Google voice – I am torn on this one, as I love the potential of Google voice, but it is rude when it asks me my name before it rings, and it is even worse when you do not pick-up because now I think that you have screened the call. Perhaps it is a paranoia thing or something.

Be Prepared

For this interview, being prepared is the name of the game. You should have your resume out in front of you as well as a copy of the job description for the position you are interviewing for. You should have studied BOTH – highlight the items on the job description that help you stand out as a candidate and be sure that you hit those points during the call.

During this interview, you will be asked about your background, your experience, why you are interested in the position, what makes you interested in the company, and essentially why you should be considered for this role. Mind you, if they are good at their job, recruiters will not necessarily ask those questions outright. But that is the kind of information they are seeking. Do you have the skills for the position? In addition, they will be listening for underlying clues about who you are as a person. Can you communicate your thoughts clearly, are you organized, have you done your homework, are you someone that they want to work with, would you fit into the company culture? And so on.

Chat with a Friend

The people that excel during phone interviews are the people who are clear communicators. They are ready for all of the questions they are asked, they do not deliver rehearsed answers, and the recruiter leaves the conversation feeling as though they got to know the candidate thoroughly – it feels like they were chatting with a friend. It is all about staying calm, cool and collected – and answering each question fully, concisely.

In other words, the interviewee engages me in a conversation. I am still doing most of the asking, and they are doing most of the talking, but it becomes a conversation instead of another treacherous rote interview. Before your phone interview, think about how you would interact with your friend – and then approach the interview in the same way. TALK to the recruiter about what you do, how you do it, and why you love it – your enthusiasm and comfort with your experience and their position, will win you an opportunity in the next round.

General Best Practices:

- **If you are sick, if you lost your voice, if you are at the doctor's office, or generally unwell, please reschedule your interview.** Honestly, people – I literally had someone try to do a phone interview when he sounded like he was on his death bed. He could not hear my questions and he clearly was napping when I called during our scheduled time. I asked him several times if he wanted to reschedule (hint: that is a sign to say "yes"), and he refused. Needless to say, he did not make it to the next round, but perhaps he could have been a perfect fit. Who knows? Nine times out of ten, it will not be an issue to simply admit to your illness and reschedule the call.

- **Do not have barking dogs, crying kids, or another distractions going on in the background.** Either way, it is a general sign of how serious you are about the position and how much effort you are willing to put into the interview process. I know that sometimes these things are out of your control, but it comes across as unprofessional. And who knows, you may even offend a recruiter who is not fond of such cuteness.

- **Schedule the call when you have a significant time gap, in case the call goes long or starts late.** You do not need to block out your entire day for a 30-minute phone interview, but just try and give yourself a 15-minute window of wiggle room on each side. If the conversation is flowing nicely, do not create a scenario where you have to hang up to run to another meeting abruptly.

- **Only answer questions that you feel comfortable with.** I will not mention any names, but I know a few people who try to go outside of the bounds during a phone interview. I believe it is unintentional, but if you feel as though a line has been crossed, it is ok to simply pass on the question. Know your rights and appropriate interview questions before starting the process. You do not have to answer (and you should not even be asked), questions about your spouse/significant other/etc.; what your spouse or parents do for a living; how many kids you have; when you think you will start having kids; where you are from; and so on. I have included this handy set of interview guidelines to help you. Just be sure to decline to answer with grace, class and maybe a little humor to try and direct the interview back on track.

- **Know what your salary requirements are.** This is the most obvious place for this question to first pop up, so make sure you have done some research and have a range in mind. I recommend having a range around $15,000, if appropriate (or a range of $5 for an hourly position). I would always recommend framing your answer like this:

> "My current salary requirements are between $XXk and $XXk, although I am open to discussing how my range meets the guidelines for this position."

You are able to state your requirements, but also not knock yourself out of the running should there be a huge discrepancy. If they respond with something like, "that's well outside of the acceptable range for this position," you have a decision to make. Either lower your salary requirement standards, or move on to another position. But know firmly, that you will NOT be receiving the salary that you requested.

Skype Interviews

Being able to visually see someone during an interview is a great opportunity for the recruiter to "kill two birds with one stone." Part of the lore of doing Skype interviews for recruiters, is that the interviews are very uncomfortable. I am not going to lie – I think it is super strange when you are interviewing someone and seeing someone in their own personal space. But it also allows the recruiter, to see your body language and more fully understand your intent with each response.

I have had a handful of Skype interviews, and they are typically *not* the first interaction you have with the company, which is good news. But they are more stressful than a typical phone interview. You have to worry about your hair, your make-up, the technology, and where to look! But, a Skype interview can really work in your favor. You are able to get across so much more about who you are live via video versus a phone call. Be you, let your personality shine through, and remain calm at all costs. It is awkward and surreal at first – how you manage that, is exactly what they are looking for. Remember what recruiters are trying to gauge from you: your skills, your personality, how you engage others under pressure, what your "space" looks and feels like, cultural fit with the hiring manager and company, and your skills.

Best Practices

- **Do a test run. Before every single interview.** I cannot stress this enough. Just because Skype worked perfectly yesterday, does not mean that it will be functional when you need it (speaking from experience here). Do a quick video chat with a friend about 20 minutes before your interview to test everything out, so you are set to go before the interview.
- **Keep your Skype name professional**. The same principles apply here as using a ridiculous email address. Use your name or some variation of it, to make it easy and professional. If you have to set-up a new "job interview/professional" account, do it – it is simple and free.
- **Pay attention to your background setting.** Since we typically Skype with friends and family, our surroundings are usually not the main focus. But remember, just like a phone interview, this is an impression situation. You only have a few seconds to make the strongest impression via the screen, so make sure that you have planned everything. You do not need to redo your office to make it designer-ready, just remove any offensive materials behind you. Think: posters, post-it notes, clutter, and so on. Test what is seen through your webcam and make sure it looks decent and comes off as professional, clean and put together.
- **Professional on the top, party on the bottom.** Just like a mullet, your shirt (top) needs to be business professional clothes, but there can be a party in back (bottom). This is an INTERVIEW. Wear a top that you would wear to an in-person interview such as a suit coat, button-up, etc. No one can see below your waist, so no need to go all out. It actually helps me calm down knowing that I am wearing silly pajama pants with a blazer. Do not forget that this interview should be taken seriously and make sure your top-half is groomed accordingly.
- **Figure out where to look.** Skype is strange – it is hard to figure out where you are supposed to look on the screen. If

you look at the person on your screen, you are looking down to the person on the other side. That's ok – the person on the other side is struggling with the same thing as well. I would advise sitting a bit further away from the camera (if you can), so you can do a better job at looking at the camera and the person. If you need to choose one, I tend to vote for looking at the camera. It is easier to make a connection on the other end and is closest to eye contact in an in-person conversation.

- **Remember there is a camera on.** I am sure you have all heard the funny and scary things that have been captured on a webcam when the owner forgot the camera was on. Do not be one of those videos on YouTube. Please. Right before and right after the interview, people tend to forget that they are on candid camera and either say or do silly things, forgetting that someone is on the other line. I have seen people fixing their hair, flossing, using the webcam like a mirror to make sure they are prettied up, commenting on how it went (or their opinion about the interviewer… ahem, me), and so on. Remember that the camera is on and someone is watching you. Wow, that just turned a bit Big Brother, but I think you know what I mean.

Onsite Interviews

Yay! You are officially considered a strong and viable candidate for the position – you have been asked to enter the inner sanctum of the company and meet with the important peeps. Awesome job, but now is the important part – time to make a lasting and good impression on all of the people you meet with. No pressure or anything. ;)

Basic Tactics

There are so many potential road blocks during the onsite interview process, but hopefully these basic guidelines will help you with the most obvious stumbles.

- **Ditch the nerves.** Everyone gets jitters when they are about to walk into the lion's den and interview with their potential dream job position. But your nerves will be the leading reason why you do not land the job – they are doing you no good. Instead of getting worked up about the interview and feeling unprepared, go into the interview as though you are going to talk to one of your parent's friends – be ready to tell them what you do for a living. The more you can think of the interview itself as a conversation, the better off you are. You are not going in to meet royalty – the interviewer is a person, at work. It is that simple. You know what being at work feels like, so approach accordingly.
- **Have questions about the company ready to go.** So many people do a Google search and come up with "the best questions to ask during an interview." Guess what? The three hundred people before you asked those same questions last week. Have REAL questions prepared to ask during the interview process. Remember, you are interviewing the company just as much as they are interviewing you, so ask things that would help you make the decision if you are offered the position. What is important to you to know before you step into a new situation? What types of employee perks are offered? What is valued most at the company? How are the company's values actually applied every day? What does their performance management process look like? How are internal employees provided with learning opportunities and growth potential? How many hours are expected in the position? How are benefits managed? And so on – I think you get the drift here. Ask questions that actually MEAN something to you.
- **Your arrival time matters.** I am not quite sure what is going on lately, but so many people are arriving to their interviews either late or way too early. Either way, this is not the first impression you want to provide your potential employer. When you know you are going to be late due to unforeseen obstacles (traffic is a lame excuse – be sure to give yourself more than enough time to make it there), call the interviewer

immediately. There is nothing worse than showing up late without some advance notice. And almost as bad, is arriving too early. Put yourself in the interviewer's shoes – they have meetings, things booked all day long. While your interview is a big deal to you, it is just another meeting for him/her. So when you get there super early, they have to stop everything they are doing to attend to you (or at the very least, they feel pressured to do so). Make sure you walk through the front door ten minutes before your interview. If you have to sit in your car for 30 minutes beforehand, do that please (no one is watching you).

- **Dress to impress.** I know I talk about this a lot, but apparently there are still some questions as to what is work appropriate (based on what you all are wearing!). Regardless of the type of company you are going to, please dress up – wear a suit or equally appropriate attire. Do not wear revealing tops (no cleavage people, at all) and wear skirts that cover the right things. Oh – and shoes. Men: please wear "dressy" shoes that do not look like you just walked through mud in them. Women: no hooker heels – totally inappropriate. Scale it down and lower the heel (less than three inches), particularly if you cannot walk in higher heels.
- **Do your homework.** When you are going to be meeting people onsite, you should have done your homework fully – print out a copy of the job description and know exactly what is included; review the company website; understand their mission and values; and also do some LinkedIn research on who you are meeting with. Not only will you be asked about all of these things in one way or another, you will come across as very interested in the position without having to try. My secret trick is LinkedIn research – at a minimum, search for your interviewer's name. You can find out where they have worked before, what their positions have been, and possibly find some commonalities with them (like where they went to school, clubs, etc). I like to go even further and start clicking on the "others who looked at this person also viewed" suggestions LinkedIn provides. You will get a feel

for the type of people who work at the company and also be prepared for any last minute interviewer additions.

- **Be an amplified version of yourself** (in most cases). If you are usually quiet and reserved, now is the time to break out of that shell and be more outgoing and bubbly. In my experience, the candidate who has the most experience AND is most likeable/has the most presence, is the person who ends up getting the job. The interviewer is looking for people he/she wants to work with, interact with, on a daily basis. You do not want to come across as a wallflower or overly aggressive. You want to be concise, confident and engaging at all levels.

Expect the Unexpected

You *never* know what is going to happen once you step foot onsite at a company. In my own interviewing history, I was put in the following situations (just to name a few):

- I was told I was coming onsite to present a strategy to the owners. After I presented the strategy, they invited their entire senior staff (10 people) into the room for me to deliver it to them and answer any/all of their questions. People: they scheduled me for a 30 minute onsite interview that ended up lasting almost two hours, meeting with the owners to all staff members.
- I was scheduled to meet with four interviewers onsite, but two did not make the flight down, so instead I had two phone interviews while sitting in one of the company's conference rooms.
- An in-person interview turned into a live video conference interview with two interviewers in the room, instead of the onsite one-on-one interview I was expecting.
- A scheduled interviewer was out of the office, so they had me meet with the incumbent, who was, we'll say, not pleased

they were replacing her position. Oh, and I did get that job and had to work with her…

I have several more examples, but I think you get the point. You must be prepared for the unforeseen things that pop-up during the interview process. I am not going to say that HR does these things as a test, but how you respond to them is absolutely being judged. Interviewing is not comfortable to begin with, but it is even more difficult when crinkles happen. How you respond under pressure is very telling to how well you can handle the position and how you fit into the company culture. So the unexpected is good, just be cognizant of how you react to it.

The best way to react to the unexpected during the interview process is to be calm and collected. Showing displeasure, annoyance, or downright disgust will not win you any points (even if all of those things are true). It is time to be an actor and take a deep breath before reacting. The more you can roll with the punches, the better – and it will help you stand out, especially if the situations were particularly unforeseen or difficult (the team will have sympathy for you and may even comment on how well you managed the situation).

Sure-Fire Ways to Knock Yourself Out of the Running

I wish that this were not the case, but there are so many ways to mess up the onsite interview process. As a whole, they are trying to weed people out, not nominate people in. I have explained several ways to help your cause above, but there are also sure-fire ways to be eliminated during the interview process. And no, these are not all-inclusive, but they are the most common reasons why I have seen candidates not be asked to continue in the process.

- By **not following any of the advice above** (showing up at the wrong time, not wearing professional clothing, not being prepared, and so on – follow that guidance!).
- They **talked too much**. Seriously – stop talking, and allow the interview team to have a conversation with you.

- They were **too relaxed with their posture and answers**. Even if you create a connection with the hiring team, (which is awesome!) you are still not a *part* of the team yet. So coming across as too relaxed has been the demise to many candidates.

- **Inappropriate jokes or comments** during the interview. Um, it is NEVER ok to curse during an interview, even if your interviewer does (oh, the stories I could tell you on this topic). But your responses should remain professional. And for the love of Nancy, do not make any type of off-topic comments or joke. We had to pass on a super strong candidate because he "offended" one of the interviewers with one of his comments.

- **Being rude to the receptionist, HR or any other staff** you come into contact with. They have a direct line to the hiring team, so do not treat them like "the help." Perhaps we can just say you should treat ALL people with respect? Just saying…

- **Speaking poorly of your previous employer**. If you are speaking badly about them, people immediately think sour grapes and that you would speak poorly about their company. Just don't do it.

- **Not showing enthusiasm or excitement for the job or company**. I get it, some jobs/companies are not really that exciting. They are a means to an end, or perhaps you are practicing your interview techniques. Regardless, the people who work there DO THINK that their company is pretty great. Maybe not really, but during the interview process, it is personally offensive if you are not as engaged or excited as they are about the opportunity. Lose the entitlement people.

- Generally, **not having your sh*t together**. Being disorganized, unprepared, or disheveled in general. It is hard to articulate exactly what this looks like, but we have all seen those people. Hair ruffled, resumes not printed, homework/background research not done, wrinkles in their clothes, and so on. There really is no excuse. Get yourself together and present your best foot forward.

Following Up and Thank You

You absolutely MUST follow-up after an onsite interview: with every single person you met with individually. Your thank you message can be short and sweet, but should indicate that you appreciate the time they took out of their day to meet with you, and touch upon one key discussion point you had during the process. And your thank you email should go out no later than the following morning – less than 24 hours after the interview. And if you want to make an outstanding impression, snail-mail a handwritten note to the hiring manager (this is in addition to the emailed thank you note). This personal touch goes a LONG way.

Post interview, let the recruiter drive the bus. For at least one week post interview, **do not call the recruiter. He/she will call you. HONESTLY.** And if you are wondering…"What should I do – I haven't heard back from the recruiter for the job I interviewed with (enter time-frame) ago?"

One BIG thing to keep in mind, regardless: if it has been any longer than two weeks (being generous there), without the recruiter at least touching base (and they did not let you know ahead of time that there would a significant delay in the process), it is pretty safe to say that you have not been chosen for that job. More specifically, it is because of one of these reasons:

You Are Not Their Top Candidate

Companies tend to find two candidates that they could "live with" in any given position. There is usually a stand-out, or the preferred top candidate, and then a "we can do with that" person. Both are high performers and fully qualified for the job, but one candidate tends to be better "liked" or "fit more within the culture," and thereby becomes the desired candidate. But the most important thing for the recruiter is to fill the position, while keeping a back-up securely in place… in case the top candidate rejects the offer. You may not be hearing back from the recruiter because they are waiting to hear an acceptance or rejection from another candidate.

What should you do? Do not be discouraged, especially if it is a position you really want. You should reach out to the recruiter via email, continuing to express your interest in the position and ask for an updated timeline. Let them know that you will be continuing on your own job hunt in the meantime and do not be pushy.

Email something like: "Hi Sally, Thank you again for coordinating all of my interviews through the recruiting process. I wanted to reach out and let you know that I am still very interested in the position and am curious about what the hiring process time frame is looking like. In the meantime, I will be sure to let you know if another offer comes through as I continue on my search. Please let me know if you or the team needs any additional information/collateral from me, during this process. Best, Job Seeker."

How do you know this is the case? If you have gone through several interviews (at least two in-person interviews), felt as though you hit it off well with the team and had a once-engaged recruiter who now is slightly evasive or hard to reach.

Your Recruiter Does Not Like Delivering Bad News

I hate to say this, but put yourself in the recruiter's shoes. It is extremely difficult to have to tell qualified (and nice, kind, funny, etc.) candidates that they have not been chosen for the position. And they have to tell so many people, each day. Sometimes, especially if you connected, they just ignore the "no" pile until they are pushed to do so (as in, a candidate corners them). It can get extremely uncomfortable when a candidate asks for feedback when the recruiter is delivering "the no," as the feedback they typically receive from the hiring manager is unsuitable to pass along or they disagree with the decision. So instead, they ignore the situation altogether.

What should you do? If you have already sent an email to the recruiter asking for status and have heard no response, it is time to move on. One email is sufficient enough following an in-person interview. They know who you are and where you are in the process, so if they are not responding to you, move on. Do not stalk them. Do not try and ask for any type of feedback or what went wrong at this point. Just move on and keep applying elsewhere.

How do you know this is the case? Most likely you have had a good connection with the recruiter throughout the process and then you cannot get a response from them. You may have had an awkward closing meeting during your last interview or felt something a little off during the process. And above all else, you are not getting a straight answer or suddenly have radio silence.

The Hiring Manager is Dragging His/Her Feet

This is often the case and, unfortunately, out of the hands of the recruiter. It is hard to share any news, when the recruiter does not have any to share, especially when someone else is holding up the process. A good recruiter will continue to keep in contact with you if you are a strong candidate (it is called "keeping you hot").

What should you do? It can be very frustrating, but if it is a job that you are very interested in, hang tight (while continuing your search at other companies). It is usually not a reflection of how strong of a candidate you are (or are not), but more about the hiring manager's decision-making process or potential budget issues. Be sure to keep the conversation going with the recruiter until he/she provides additional details.

How do you know this is the case? The recruiter is reaching out to you or responding to your emails, but there is no real information included. They are trying to push out the hiring timeline, but not giving you specifics or any new information about the process.

Chapter 7 – The Offer

* * *

Oh my gosh! You have made it through the most difficult part of the process and have secured an offer!!! But before you start celebrating, it is time to get to work. Hammering out your offer is a critical part of the hiring process and one that will have long-lasting effects to your career. Many people, including me, loathe the thought of negotiating, especially when it comes to money. But one thing is certain – you must absolutely negotiate your offer (I learned this the hard way).

The Offer Process

The offer itself will be different depending upon the company extending the offer to you, but the process is fairly similar. You will (hopefully) receive a phone call from the recruiter or the hiring manager, following your last interview. They will be eager to chat with you to extend the news and cross the position off of their own to-do lists. If you miss the call (please try not to), they will leave you a message without spilling the beans, so do not read too much into that. Typically a verbal offer is extended during the call, followed by a written offer. You should NEVER accept the offer during the first conversation (more on this later). You will then need to get back to the recruiter/hiring manager with your answer and send along the signed offer packet and confirm your start date. Once HR has received your signed documents, the necessary background checks will be completed (and your offer will be contingent upon this).

The process itself is usually swift. If it drags out for more than a week or two, something is wrong. The most important part of the process is being available for discussion, having clear and realistic expectations, and continuing to be a pleasure to work with. Nothing is 100% secure. I have seen people's offers rescinded because they were jerks during negotiation, the hiring manager changed their mind, or something popped up during the background check.

Reference Checks

Having your references ready for a call is a necessary evil of the offer process. Reference checking is an outdated process and one that is sometimes ignored altogether, depending upon the company (although they will always ask for them). The idea behind checking your references is to gauge your overall performance and personality from a previous coworker's first-hand experience. Before social media networking sites, this process provided a lot more value. Nowadays, speaking to your references is somewhat insignificant. Why?

1. The hiring manager has already chosen you as his/her best choice. They have talked to too many candidates to just turn the other way and start the process over. See how important winning them over is?
2. People only provide references that they got along with. No one in their right mind is going to put down a former nemesis as a reference.
3. People can be sued for providing negative feedback about a former colleague/employee. So no one is really willing to share the truth.
4. Most companies have a "no reference" rule in place, although many people do not abide by them. This is so HR can monitor employment checks and provide only middle of the road (legally satisfying) information.

But regardless of your references' significance, you need to have them ready to go. Some companies will ask for specific types of references based on their own needs, but here are the types of references that you should have at the ready, at a minimum.

- Former manager (at least one, two is preferable)
- Former client (have two ready)
- Former colleague (have two ready at different levels if possible – one peer, one above in level, etc.)

- Former direct report (if you have ever managed anyone and the position also has direct reports, then you need to have at least one of your former direct reports ready to speak on your behalf)

Then what? Well, if they are anything like me, the recruiter will do some research on you by way of LinkedIn. This is especially true for higher-level positions, but can be applied to all positions. Here is what I do… I take the list of references that you have provided me with and follow-up with them if they are applicable. Then I search LinkedIn and find out who you have intentionally left off the list. For instance, if you reported to the CEO at your last job but have not included the CEO in your list of references, that will absolutely make me suspicious. So I will reach out to that person to try and figure out why via a reference check. This is a lot of work for non-senior positions, but for positions with high-visibility, the extra-legwork pays off.

Choose your references wisely and make sure that they are aware that they are references before you add them to your list. And notice how I keep mentioning "have them ready to go?" The worst thing you can do when it comes to reference checks is making the hiring manager wait to get your list. It seems as though you have to quickly find *someone* to speak highly of you. So when asked, send them over immediately. Oh, and quick note – do not send references until a) you are asked for them and b) you have met onsite with the team and are at the closing stage of the interview process.

Negotiate Me Baby

Employment offers in government and academic jobs, usually have a strictly stated pay range and there is not much negotiating room during the offer process. However, for just about every other sector, you absolutely should NOT accept the first offer HR throws your way. Instead, negotiate, my friend!

I do want to note that there are times where you may not get anywhere through negotiations. Perhaps the recruiter has extended their best and final offer during the conversation, or perhaps the company just does not have anything else in the well. That is OK – I would still recommend *asking* for more, just continue to be careful about your approach! If you come across as too aggressive or overzealous, it can easily turn off a hesitant company that feels as though they have delivered a strong package.

1. Remember that HR is looking out for the good of the company first. So they will absolutely **try and get every employee at the lowest investment** – that just makes good business sense. If you provided them a range during the interview process that you would accept, they will probably put your offer at the low-end of that range.
2. **Do not pass on the offer without asking for more.** This happens all of the time and is usually delivered via email (stop that, people). "I'm sorry, I'm not going to be able to accept that offer. It will not meet my salary requirements to pay my bills or cover the commute." I think you get the drift here and the stories I have heard have been hilarious. Anyway, these candidates threw in the towel before exploring what else could be available to them and missed out on good job opportunities.
3. **You should always ask for more, but how you do it will greatly impact your reputation at the company**. For example, I once offered a position to "John" for an entry-level position with a very decent base salary plus commission. He had zero experience and did not even have a desired starting salary. Following me? Well, he came back asking for more money and did it aggressively – basically, he said that he could get a better offer elsewhere and that he would refuse to take the offer and would rather find a new job. So… when the hiring manager asked me how the offer conversation went, I parlayed the information along (greatly toned down), and let him know that he wanted $10k more on his base salary before he would even consider the position. Can you guess what the hiring manager's response was? He told me to rescind the offer and that John would no longer be

considered a candidate. John's pushiness came across as greedy and not excited to join *our* team. Not the impression you want to precede you before you start a new position.

There is not a one-size-fits-all for counter offers, but based on the many successful (and unsuccessful) offers that I have been a part of, below is a good script for you to use when you have been offered a new position. Oh, and be sure to do this at least over the phone (not on email!).

Script for Negotiation

Recruiter (Bob): "Hi Jill, we are so excited to be able to extend you an offer of employment here at ABC. Your starting base salary will be $30k with an annual bonus and partially paid benefits."

Jill (YOU): "Bob – that's fantastic news. I have enjoyed getting to know everyone and more about the company during the interview process and am very excited to join the ABC team. Can you tell me more about the benefits?"

Recruiter: "Sure we offer…."

Jill (YOU): "Sounds like an interesting package. I would like to take some to consider the offer as a whole. Can I get back to you within 24 hours?"

> Note: If they say no, then run very far away from the company. If they are not willing to let you have some time to work the numbers and make a huge life decision, then there is a problem. Be thankful that you found out before it was too late. If they say yes, then proceed.

Jill (YOU): "Thank you – I appreciate you allowing me the opportunity to fully evaluate the numbers and the package and ensure that I am making a great decision."

Note: You have two options – you review the offer and come back the next day asking for more, or you can nudge the envelope a little here. Personally, I think it is easier to do that during this first call as you are already talking about numbers and do not have to initiate another call, but it's a personal decision.

Jill (YOU): "Bob, $30k seems a little bit low for the position and my experience. I have been interviewing for positions that have come with a slightly higher base salary. Is there any room for negotiation here? I had been hoping for the offer to be at $37 – $40k." THEN STOP TALKING

Note: If you are quiet, the recruiter will pick up the conversation from there. You have asked for what you wanted, and now it is up to them to seek out the details. They should not say "no" immediately. Usually they check back with the hiring manager or will have the ability to go up on the spot. If they push back with a "that's not going to happen," then I would ask for them to circle back with the hiring manager or know that the base salary is not open for negotiation… but other things may be, so ask.

What's Up for Negotiation?

Literally, almost everything is up for negotiation. I have seen people negotiate benefit premiums, stock awards, annual bonus percentage or target, incentive program, office space, telecommute options, vacation time, and so on. Your base salary is not the only thing that can be altered during the offer, but it is the best time to get the best deal.

Remember, this is the *only* time during your employment that you will be able to set a baseline of your compensation package – what you negotiate here will be your starting point going forward and quite difficult to change once you have officially joined the team. Think about all of the things that will help you get what you want out of the job, and go after it.

Things to Consider Before Accepting an Offer

Accepting any job is a personal decision, sometimes even a family decision. Far too often I see candidates accepting a job either out of desperation or from ignorance. A new job is a huge life decision and should be considered as such. Knowing what to ask and what to consider before saying "yes" or "no" is a helpful tool when making this decision. These are all of the things that I wish I knew before starting a new position (in no particular order).

- Compensation: Know your exact base salary, the payroll schedule, bonus opportunities (the target amount and how it is calculated, as well as previous years' payouts).
- Vacation Time: Understand the vacation or Paid Time Off (PTO) policies. Know the number of days, how it is calculated, any restrictions (some companies have a "one-week off at a time" policy), how often vacation is taken, holiday schedule, and so on.
- Hierarchy Structure (especially if title is important to you): Understanding, before you accept a new position and title, how the company is structured is important. I remember getting roped into a position with a "high title" in a previous organization, which was actually lower than my experience level within that organization. Each company is different, so be sure to ask how the titles are structured.
- General Company Information: Company size, years in business, mission and values, any available earnings statements, and so on. Fully know what you are getting yourself into before you make the leap. Sometimes a little digging can be helpful in deciding if a company has the same ethical standards or personality that you are looking for.
- Perks: Most companies have some kind of perks, but you need to ask. Will you get stock options? Do they give out spot awards? Do you get discounts to places around the city?

And so on. Find out everything that the company has to offer so you can include those items in your decision.

- Company Culture: What is valued at the company? How the company works (in teams or as individuals)? How do they celebrate their employees? What type of community involvement do they have? And so on. Understand what your everyday will be like before stepping into the role.
- Turn Over, Retention Rate, Growth: These are HUGE things to know about before you walk in the door, and the only people who are typically asking are future HR employees. You absolutely MUST know the company's turnover rate. This is a percentage of the number of employees who leave the organization. If it is any higher than 10%: Houston, we have a problem. Turnover rates can indicate overall employee satisfaction (including how they feel about management, their pay, the company culture, and so on). Each industry varies, but in this economy, a 10% turnover is fairly high. Another metric is the retention rate. This is a percentage of the number of employees who have left the company voluntarily – a bit different than the turnover rate. Essentially, this shows people who are leaving because they found something better. I would be concerned if it was any higher than 7 – 10%. And finally, growth – this indicates the company's expansion. How many new employees have they added in the last year, not as replacements, but as new positions? This will help you determine the company's viability in the long-run.

Decision Time

You have asked and they have answered all of your questions, they have spoken to your references, you have negotiated your little heart out. Now it is time for you to make the big decision! Hopefully you are still excited to join their team after the process – sometimes the process itself is a way to weed out the company. That being said, before you sign on the dotted line, make sure you have the following in writing:

- Start date
- Your manager's name and title
- Your official title
- Your salary information – base salary, any bonus targets with payout date information and calculations
- Payroll schedule (every two weeks, twice a month, etc.)
- Vacation information – number of days allotted each year, if they rollover, and how they are prorated for your start date
- Comprehensive benefits information – medical plans, amount or percentage that the company pays, what you will be responsible for covering each month, 401k or other employer-sponsored savings program, matching opportunities, tuition reimbursement, stock options, pension plan, and so on.
- Company information including your work hours, your job description and expectations in the role, ethics policy, employee handbook

Feel comfortable about what you are getting yourself into? Fantastic!!! Sign away and plan your first day at your new job. Congratulations – now it is time to celebrate!

And a little note for your sanity: The first rule of a new job is that it is going to take time to adjust to it. I know we all fantasize that our dream job will immediately be the best thing that has ever happened to us. It will suck. Plain and simple, even if you landed an awesome job, transitioning into it will take time, work, and a lot of adjustment. Just be sure to hang in there as you transition into a new adventure. Keep your mind open and give yourself about three months, at least, to start forming any opinions about the company/job/people. Yes, it really does take that long before you can make an educated decision either way.

Chapter 8 – What are the Odds?

* * *

This is the "miscellaneous" chapter of advice and odds and ends. Consider it general job-landing advice to help you through some of the dips during the process.

Not Getting the Offer

Going through the entire interview process, being a final candidate, and not getting the offer is the most frustrating position to be in, especially when you *know* how amazing you would be in that job. Unfortunately, it does happen. How you move forward following this disappointment, will greatly increase your chances of finally *getting* the offer.

The first thing you need to reflect on is what went wrong during the process or what needs additional attention before you set out on your hunt again. Hopefully the guide below will help you adjust when needed, and get back on track.

Troubleshooting Guide

Stop Point	Action Needed
Not getting phone interviews	This is a strong indication that your resume and resume materials are not properly suited for the positions you are applying for. The best way to find this out quickly is to request a resume critique (I do these for $25 – just send me an email request) to find out what professionals see when they look at your resume (or what they don't see). Another thing to consider is the type and level of jobs that you are applying to and your application techniques. If you are only applying to large companies via their online portals, then your approach should be adjusted as well (think: different kinds of companies and a more personal touch).
Not getting past the phone interview	This means your phone skills need some work. For whatever reason, you are not great at communicating about yourself, your experience, your excitement, and so on, during a phone interview. This is a show-stopper – you must absolutely work on this. Being able to deliver a good phone interview will open many doors for you, and will hold you back from ever moving forward if you do this poorly. Review all of the tips I have included above, but more importantly, do mock phone interviews with your friends and family and then get their feedback. Start by asking: how did I sound, how was the call quality, what stood out to you, what key qualifications did you take-away from our call, did I talk too much, what was your overall impression? Then get to work at improving!
Not getting past the first in-person	It should be no secret to you any longer, that doing well in an interview is all about how well you sell yourself. If you do not get asked to come back following the first interview, it is time to up your in-

interview	person presence. To start, you may not have brought enough enthusiasm or the "nice guy" factor. You most likely did not present the desired qualities – someone they want to work with (likeability) combined with the smart (but not threatening) factor. Work on how you can balance this going forward. Also, make sure you are presenting yourself properly, visually. This takes practice. Work with your friends or mentor, to figure out where you are going wrong. Ask your practice buddy the following: did I talk too much, was I clear and concise in my answers, did I provide STAR examples for each question, how could I improve, did I prove my competence?
Not getting the offer	If you have made it several rounds in the process, but not getting the offer, this is most likely more about the cultural fit or "likability" factor of another candidate. This is usually not as much of a personal reflection of you, than the position and company. If you feel as though you did well, then I would stick with that experience and try and find ways that you can still improve for the next go. The important thing is to know that you got very far in the process and do not let this one opportunity get you down.

When to Bring in the Big Guns

There are a few clear signs that it is time to bring in hired help to work with you to land a job. Sometimes it is because they can provide expert guidance, such as redoing your resume, and other times it is to help you see what needs to be improved. While there are no hard and fast rules to this, here are some guidelines of when to call in help.

- You have been searching for a new job for longer than three months.

- You are not getting past the application or phone interview stages.
- You are trying to change industries or functions.
- You are not sure what your next career step should be.
- You are stuck in analysis paralysis about the process and not moving forward.

Don't Make these Mistakes

I have outlined the most common stumbling blocks along the way and how to avoid each and every one. But there are a few general mistakes that will prevent you from finally securing the job you want.

Stop being an egomaniac. I know, this is at least the second time that I have tried to ego-check you, but getting in your own way is the most common thing holding you back from fully realizing your potential. As people, we like to stay firmly in our comfort zone and do things that make us feel as accomplished as possible. The problem is that in order to grow and learn, you have to be open to experience new things. Opening your mind to new types of jobs, companies, duties, and titles, will allow you to expand your reach while leveraging your unique talents.

Quit the blame game. Plain and simple: if you have not landed a job after searching for a few months, you are doing something not quite right. I cannot tell you how many times I hear job hunters blame a bad economy. Right now it may be a very tough job market, but there is always a war for qualified and intelligent talent going on. Since 2008, I cannot even count the number of positions, because it is too high, that have sat unfilled because we were unable to find qualified candidates, and these were not niche positions! There are jobs out there, great jobs even, but until you stop identifying with "general woes," you will not be able to see the opportunities right in front of you.

Stop being idle and stagnant. I get it, you feel a bit disillusioned with the whole process, and dare I say, frustrated. But once you step off the bus, it continues forward without you. The absolute worst thing you can do is "take a break" or give up completely on your job search. I know that it can seem a bit like Sisyphus's tale at times (like you are constantly pushing a rock uphill), but each action you take brings you closer to success – so keep on trekking up the hill.

Chapter 9 – Get Your Ass in Gear Now

* * *

It is time to get amped! Hopefully you have been taking action at each step along the way, but if not, now is the time to stop reading and start DOING. Simply reading about what happens behind the scenes secrets of how to land a job will not be enough to make it happen. It is time to get off your ass and get into gear.

If you are feeling a bit overwhelmed by how much work it takes, all you need to do is start with this: **follow the checklist provided**. That is it – you do not need to do anything else, but complete each activity along the way. Change, progress, awesomeness, and dreams are accomplished not by big actions, but by the small steps we take along the way.

You deserve to land the job of your dreams. You are worth it and you are more than qualified. Go after it baby!

Checklist of Action

Social Media:

- ☐ Google Yourself – address any necessary items
- ☐ Clean up your Facebook account and make it private
- ☐ LinkedIn: create and update your profile, find your friends, remove your current manager
- ☐ Check out additional social media sites (Twitter, Instagram, Pinterest); make sure they are set to private and do not contain any non-professional items

Be Clear About the Job You are Seeking:

- ☐ Determine your skills using the skill-finding template
- ☐ Clearly define what you are trying to fix, escape, or improve
- ☐ Dream your ideal work conditions
- ☐ Reality check – what skills do you possess and what level are you really at? (review skill-level job title tool)

Resume:

- ☐ Check your ego
- ☐ Pick your specialization
- ☐ Start selling yourself… or at least thinking like a salesman
- ☐ Practical tactical review
- ☐ Cover letter

Search and Apply:

- ☐ Get online and try new and proven sites
- ☐ Go local
- ☐ Apply like you are an ATS (applicant tracking system)

Interviewing:

- ☐ Stand out like a STAR
- ☐ Become an interview master

The Offer:

- ☐ References ready to go
- ☐ Practice your negotiation script
- ☐ Ask all of the offer considerations and questions

What are the Odds:

- ☐ Evaluate your progress and determine where things are breaking down for improvement

Thank You!

And now I'd like to ask your help to spread the love:

1. If you have learned something from this book and have your own job-landing story to tell, I want to hear about it! Please leave a comment on my site at Loosen Your White Collar.
2. If you know of anyone who desperately needs to land a job, please tell them about to visit Loosen Your White Collar to sign-up for my free newsletter and to learn more about the book.

Full of landing-love,
Melissa

e: melissa@loosenyourwhitecollar.com
w: http://loosenyourwhitecollar.com
t: @mellymelanz
f: http://facebook.com/loosenyourwhitecollar

www.ingramcontent.com/pod-product-compliance
Lightning Source LLC
Chambersburg PA
CBHW060632210326
41520CB00010B/1575

* 9 7 8 0 6 1 5 7 0 8 3 8 6 *